Beer and Cider in Ireland
The Complete Guide

Iorwerth Griffiths

LIB
ERT
IES

First published in 2007 by
Liberties Press
Guinness Enterprise Centre | Taylor's Lane | Dublin 8 | Ireland
T: +353 (1) 415 1224
E: info@libertiespress.com
W: www.libertiespress.com

Liberties Press is a member of Clé, the Irish Book Publishers' Association

Trade enquiries to CMD Distribution
55a Spruce Avenue | Stillorgan Industrial Park | Blackrock | County Dublin
Tel: +353 (1) 294 2560 | Fax: +353 (1) 294 2564

ISBN: 978–1–905483–17–4

2 4 6 8 10 9 7 5 3 1

A CIP record for this title is available from the British Library

Designed and typeset by Ros Murphy
Map by Vidhya Mohankumar
Printed by Castuera, Navarra, Spain

The Irish tradition of brewing is a very ancient one and we have contributed one of the great beers to the world in the form of the distinctive and iconic stout known as Guinness. But there's more to Irish beer than the famous black gold of St James's Gate.

Could we have said that twenty years ago? Frankly, no. The twentieth century was not kind to Irish brewing or to consumer choice. One by one, the regional breweries closed or were consumed by larger entities in which their particular brews became submerged.

Our national poverty didn't help. In straitened times, who was going to challenge the dominance of the big, internationally owned brands? Odd as it may seem, there were people who did – I'm thinking of Oliver Hughes and Liam La Hart who went on to found The Porterhouse – but the times were not propitious.

Ireland's economic boom came just after the renaissance of craft brewing in Britain during the 1980s and we were fortunate to be able to tap into the expertise that had been developed there, notably through the missionary zeal and utter passion of Brendan Dobbin.

Greater prosperity has brought huge changes to consumer behaviour, not all of them very edifying; but a well-heeled and well-travelled population has developed an adventurous palate and a desire to move away from the blandness that prevails in many, but not all, of the big brands.

Despite the favourable conditions for brewing in Ireland, would-be micro-brewers still require a lot of courage and a considerable amount of vision and passion. Iorwerth Griffiths has captured that spirit here. He has also given credit, when it is due, to the big operators who are so often dismissed wholesale by the beer snobs. Or should that be beer anoraks?

Guinness has been producing some astonishingly good stouts in the Brewhouse series which are available in selected outlets in Dublin, and Macardles is still one of the best Irish ales, despite being confined to the greater Dundalk area.

Irish brewing has never been more diverse and we now come to the surprising conclusion that our beers and ciders do actually merit a comprehensive guide. In the 1980s, such a guide could have been written on the back of an envelope; the appearance of this book is a very eloquent testament to the renaissance in brewing in Ireland.

We will never see Findlater's Stout or Cairne's Ale again (and to be honest, most of us never did) but Iorwerth Griffiths has much to tell us about our local beers and ciders and is not afraid to supply trenchant tasting notes. This is, quite simply, a very useful and timely book.

Tom Doorley
Conna, Co. Cork, July 2007

Ireland has a well-known love for beer, its pubs are famous throughout the world, and Irish cider is on the up again, with its image revolutionised. For all the beer and cider that is drunk, how many people know anything about the beer and cider they are drinking – how it's made, what goes into it, and what makes a good beer or cider, as opposed to the dull or plain dreadful. Take a closer look at most Irish pubs: many are fine establishments and justly celebrated, but what about the beer and cider? You will usually see the same few brands in every pub.

Thankfully things are changing, new imported beers are arriving, the Irish craft brewing scene is gathering momentum, and even new ciders are becoming available. Also, people are beginning to talk about and appreciate beer and cider in a way that in the past was deemed fit only for wine. This book introduces people to the richness and diversity of beer and cider in Ireland, the history, how they are made, who makes them, and the beers and ciders that are out there.

People go on endlessly about wine and will reach for a bottle with their meal. The wine establishment has done a great job in convincing everyone that wine is sophisticated, whereas beer is not. But the fact is that beer has a far greater spectrum of flavours, from the crisp, clean pilsner to the quenching tartness of a wheat beer, the more-ish hoppy tang of a pale ale, the malty sweetness of an Irish red ale, and the roasted richness of an Irish dry stout. This is why beer makes a better food companion than wine: it has a greater range of flavours to match your chosen dish. And this book aims to show that there is a lot more to beer than the bland mass-produced lagers the marketing people tell us we should be drinking.

Cider can also vary, depending on the apples used and how it is made. Cider can be fizzy and sweet but that is only one kind of cider. It can also be lightly sparkling or even still like wine, it can be dry and sharp, and it can be made from a single variety of apple in the way that some wines are made from a single grape variety. Cider is also an excellent food companion. Bulmers/Magners is known locally as 'Clonmel Chardonnay'. A joke, perhaps, but in countries such as France and Germany, cider is seen as an alternative to wine rather than an alternative to beer. Well-made ciders are characterful and can replace white wine at any occasion. Sprinkled throughout the book, you will find some ideas about matching beer and cider with food.

Both beer and cider are natural products. Beer is essentially malted barley, water, hops and yeast, while cider is apple juice and yeast, much like wine is grape juice and yeast. The flavour of beer predominantly comes from the type of malted barley used and the variety of hops. The flavour and feel of cider depends on the variety of apple used.

Beer and cider are also Irish drinks with long histories on this island: for instance, we know that St Patrick employed a brewer. Most towns in Ireland had one or more breweries in the nineteenth century, and cider was made on farms in the southern counties around Limerick, Tipperary, Kilkenny, Waterford and Wexford, and in the orchard county – Armagh. However, as is the case in most countries, these small breweries were eventually closed by the bigger brewers or could not compete with them. So, rather than being able to order a pint of the local brew, the same beers are available everywhere. Farmhouse cidermaking also declined as farming itself changed. Thankfully, also in common with many other countries, small breweries and cidermakers are re-appearing, making excellent locally produced beer and cider. One problem the small producers face is getting their excellent products to the marketplace and into pubs. The big companies jealously guard the beers that are sold in pubs, and this is why most pubs have the same boring old selection. This is anti-competitive and stifles the development of an interesting and diverse beer and cider scene. As one brewer put it to me, would you go to a restaurant if it was serving six dishes and every other restaurant in Ireland was also serving the same six dishes? With pubs closing all over Ireland, maybe it is time to break the mould and attract customers by offering a diverse range of beer. Some pubs are already doing this, and you will find them in this book. Pay them a visit: you won't be disappointed.

This book also offers a guide to some of the best imported beers found in Ireland. They also increase diversity and choice, opening up new drinking experiences. Many imported beers are excellent but we shouldn't fall into the trap of believing that imports are good because they are from another country, while Irish beer is passé. Some imported beers are bland and uninteresting, while most Irish craft beers are excellent and deserve a much wider audience.

Ireland is a relative latecomer to the craft-brewing scene, mainly due to the way the market is controlled by the big brewers and, until recently, the duty regime. It would be great to have a small brewer in each major town again brewing a pint of the local stuff. The duty on cider in the Republic of Ireland is the next thing to address to enable small-scale cider producers to take the drink back to its farmhouse roots. As will be seen in the book, new breweries are being planned and a new farmhouse cider has just come on to the scene in Armagh with – hopefully – more to follow. Exciting times may be ahead for drinkers in Ireland.

I have tasted every beer and cider in this book. There are no ratings because this book aims to encourage and help develop the appreciation of beer and cider in Ireland rather than to criticise. However, it should be apparent from my comments on each product which beers and ciders I think are worth exploring and which are not. If you can't get locally produced Irish beer and cider in your local pub or off-licence, ask for it anyway: the message might eventually get through.

Alcohol enjoyed in moderation is good for our health. Great-tasting beer and cider are drinks of moderation, made to be enjoyed and savoured; bland, tasteless beer is made to be drunk without thought. This book encourages you to talk about, appreciate and enjoy the beer and cider you drink in a responsible way. As one American brewer put it: 'Drink less, but drink better.'

Sláinte!

Iorwerth Griffiths

A book like this can only be written with the help of a number of people. Thanks to all the brewers, cidermakers and those working in the bigger breweries and cider mills who gave their time to facilitate my visits and numerous follow-up questions: Gerry Forrest (Árainn Mhór); Aidan Callery, D. J. Kiely and the superb Ed Hinchy – who I hope will find the time to author a work on the history of Beamish and Crawford (Beamish and Crawford); Niall Garvey (Biddy Early); Denis Hayes and Orlaith Fortune (Bulmers); Seamus and Kay O'Hara and Oonagh Diamond (Carlow); Kelly, Philip and Ann Troughton (Carsons); Dean McGuinness (Celtic Brew); Rhonda Evans (Diageo), David and Egle Llewellyn (Double L); Russell Garet and Peter Lyall (Franciscan Well); Catherine Walsh (Grayling) who organised everything regarding Bulmers and her colleague Anri McHugh; Joan Dineen and John Crowley (Heineken); Owen and Siobhan Scullion (Hilden and College Green); Aidan Murphy (Hooker); Willie Rost and John Joyce (Johnny Jump Up); David Pickering (Kinsale); Cuilan Loughnane (Messrs Maguires); Oliver Hughes, Peter Mosley and Fiona Roche (Porterhouse); Bob Little (Strangford Lough); and Bernard Sloan (Whitewater).

Thanks also and best wishes to those who will be brewing soon who responded with information about their soon-to-be-brewing breweries: Barbara-Ann McCabe in Clifden and Edward McDaid in Ramelton. And to those who have just started making excellent cider – Kenneth Redmond (Barnhill Orchards) and Sean McAteer (DARDNI) – I really hope they succeed and put Armagh back on the cider map.

Thanks to those pub managers and owners who gave up their time for a chat: Evan Doyle and Niels Toase (Actons, Macreddin); David O'Leary (Bierhaus, Cork); Jack Considine, Paul Tighe and Conor Lynam (Bierhaus, Galway); John Bittles (Bittles, Belfast); Geoff Carty (Bull and Castle, Dublin), George Greigg (Crown, Belfast); Mark McCrory (Dirty Duck); Timothy Platt (Harbour Bar, Kinsale), Peter Riley (Hillside); Martin Groundwater and David Webb (JD Wetherspoons, Northern Ireland); Pedro Donald (John Hewitt, Belfast); Benny McCabe (Mutton Lane, Oval and Sin É, Cork); Jane Bell and Dan Garth (Porterhouse, Temple Bar); Seamus Sheridan (Sheridans on the Quay, Galway); and Alison Mackintosh (Tara's, Killaloe/Ballina). Many thanks to Clare Hackett and Eibhlin Roche of the Guinness Archive and Chad Dowle of the trademark department at Diageo, London.

Thanks to John Kelly (Vertical Drinks), Greg McEllherron (Noreast Beers), Breda McGuinness (Premier Beers), Gregory McKeever (Blaney Wines) and Kate Power (Richmond Marketing).

Thanks also to Dave Jones and Dave Matthews (Cymdeithas Perai and Seidr Cymru – Welsh Perry and Cider Society), Rupert Ponsonby and Eleanor

Standen (English National Hop Association), Tony Foley (Minch Norton) and Michael Stringer (British Library).

Thanks to the publishers, Liberties Press, for believing in the idea. They have been great to work with all through this project.

A great deal of thanks to all the Mawhinneys for helping with the project in numerous ways, it would have been impossible to complete without their help.

Finally, thanks to Alison for putting up with and helping the project, me visiting breweries and tasting beer when she couldn't have any due to our daughter Annest, who arrived during the course of the research and writing of this book.

If I have forgotten anyone I sincerely apologise and promise to buy you a drink the next time we meet – as long as it's a good one!

Iorwerth Griffiths, June 2007

Horse drays at Beamish and Crawford

A SHORT HISTORY OF BREWING IN IRELAND

Beer is a true Irish drink with an ancient heritage, and Irish brewing has a history going back more than four thousand years to Celtic times.

A hundred years ago, many Irish towns had their own breweries, which produced local beer for the local population. Sadly, the history of Irish brewing has been predominantly one of the closure of breweries, or of acquisition followed by closure. As the industry contracted and concentrated in the nineteenth and twentieth centuries, competition was gradually eliminated. When a brewery closes, its beer usually disappears with it. The drinker suffers: choice is reduced, and pubs all over the country sell the same few beers. In the last ten years or so, small craft breweries, some concentrating on their locale, have appeared and many of them are making interesting brews. With people increasingly turning away from mass-produced foods and back to local produce, the future may be bright for small-scale Irish craft brewers, who are increasing choice for the beer drinker. In short, brewing in Ireland is beginning to get back to where it was a hundred years ago.

EARLY HISTORY OF BEER

The brewing of beer has its origins in the Middle East.

The first written evidence of beer is on a Sumerian tablet dating from around six thousand years ago. There is even a song entitled 'Hymn to Ninkasi – Goddess of Beer', composed around 1800 BCE. There is also a wealth of archaeological evidence to show that beer was a major industry in ancient Egypt. Brewing subsequently moved into Europe, and there is archaeological evidence that the Celts were brewing it some four thousand years ago. Their beer was a mixture of barley, oats, wheat, honey and herbs. In Celtic times in Ireland, beer was known as 'curmi', 'cormi', 'corim' or 'curim', and it is described by the Greek philosopher Discorides in 1 CE. It is also known that St Patrick himself enjoyed his 'corim', employing a priest named Mescan as his brewer.

As in other countries, in Ireland beer came under the control of the monasteries and the nobility, providing the foundation for modern brewing. Royal and noble families usually had their own brewhouses making beer for their household and court. Indeed, Richard Guinness – Arthur's father – supervised such a brewhouse in the eighteenth century.

The Críth Gablach, an Old Irish law-text on status, says that a king is expected to drink beer on Sundays with his household, and there are old mythological references to kings earning a bad reputation if their guests did not leave with the smell of beer on their breath! Other old texts, when describing the seating arrangements of royal households, make mention of a dedicated seat for the brewer, and the Seanchus Mór, a fifteenth-century text on laws and customs, describes how barley should be malted for brewing.

The beer made at this time is described as reddish in colour, and shows how Irish red ales have a connection to the past. Beer provided much-needed sustenance during the winter, when vegetables and milk were scarce: during these lean times, beer was a key source of vital minerals and vitamins.

In the monasteries, the brothers made beer for themselves and for pilgrims. Again, the sustaining qualities of beer can be discerned: brothers fasting for lent drank beer, referring to it as 'liquid bread'. With the dissolution of the monasteries in 1539, the control that had been exerted by the church and monasteries over brewing was ended, and it became a cottage industry.

FROM COTTAGE INDUSTRY TO COMMERCIAL BREWING

Until the middle of the eighteenth century, brewing in Ireland was a cottage industry mainly concentrated in the major towns and cities.

Until the middle of the eighteenth century, brewing in Ireland was a cottage industry mainly concentrated in the major towns and cities.

The brewers were usually women – 'ale wives' – and brewing was done at the same time as baking bread. Those with a reputation for brewing good ale were able to sell it, and ale-houses began to appear. The ale-house was usually a private house in which a room would be set aside for the public to purchase and drink what was essentially homebrew: an early form of what we would now call a brewpub! During this time, Irish ale was brown in colour, sweet, heavy and unhopped. It was said to be a particular favourite of King James I.

Brewing on a larger scale began to appear in the seventeenth century, and by the middle of the eighteenth century commercial brewers were beginning to distribute their ale. Domestic brewing gradually disappeared as ale-houses abandoned brewing and instead began to sell the products of the commercial brewers. This trend is echoed on a larger scale a hundred years later, when small country brewers abandoned brewing, some becoming bottlers of Guinness after finding themselves unable to compete against the Dublin giant. Several brewing dynasties were established during this time, Guinness being the most enduring.

THE BLACK STUFF

The first real revolution in the world of beer since hopped 'beer' replaced unhopped 'ale' in England in the late sixteenth and early seventeenth century was the development of porter.

This had a significant and lasting effect on the Irish brewing industry.

Porter brewing started in London in 1722, making it possible for large brewing concerns to develop. The beer of the time in England was known as 'three threads'. Publicans would serve a blend of three ales – a pale ale, a brown ale and a well-matured – or stale! –

Vats of maturing porter in the old Guinness Vathouse

brown ale. However, a brewer by the name of Ralph Harwood in Shoreditch in the East End of London created a beer with the taste and look of three threads in one barrel, called 'entire butt': an entire drink in one barrel or butt. The name changed to 'porter' over time, as this beer proved a popular drink among the market porters of Covent Garden in London.

The advent of porter brewing led to the displacement of small-scale alehouse brewing and the rise of larger-scale commercial brewers. This was due to the economies of scale that attended the new brew, as well as social change, principally a large growth in the population of London. Unlike with previous beers, porter brewing could be done on a large scale. Porter was more highly hopped, giving it a longer life, while it also benefited from a year's maturation. Both of these factors meant that it became possible – and profitable – to make a large quantity of porter and then store it in huge vats, or tuns, from which barrels would be filled as required. As the new porter beer was a single-cask product it was better suited for export than three threads. The

Shovelling out the spent grains at Guinness

closest market was Ireland, and English porter flooded in. Stronger versions were called 'stout porter', which later would become simply 'stout'. By the latter half of the eighteenth century, a quarter of all the beer drunk in Ireland was imported English porter, and Irish brewers, with their brown ale, were struggling to compete. This was due to the fact that Irish breweries of the time were small-scale and not as technologically developed as the now industrial-sized London porter brewers, such as Whitbread. Irish brewers were also hampered by a high level of duty, which the large London brewers could absorb with ease. The London porter also had the advantage of being a consistently good brew, as opposed to the variable quality of the domestic Irish ale. In 1741 imported beer amounted to 5,000 barrels; by 1793 this figure had increased to 125,000. Over a similar time period, the production of Irish brewers fell from around 178,000 barrels to 131,000, and around forty breweries closed.

Irish brewers had long been petitioning Parliament about beer duty, but their efforts had fallen on deaf ears. Finally, in 1795, Grattan repealed beer duty, and imported English porter

quickly fell away. Had beer duty not been repealed, the history of Irish brewing may have been very different indeed: Arthur Guinness was looking for suitable sites for brewing in north Wales!

Arthur Guinness had operated an ale brewery in Dublin since 1759 and was one of the first Irish brewers to switch to the production of porter in 1787, finally abandoning ale in 1799. However, the accolade of being the first porter brewer in Dublin probably goes to Thomas Andrews, who won a prize organised by the Royal Dublin Society for selling the greatest quantity of porter in a single year. The Society was keen to support Irish brewers in the face of the influx of London porter before the repeal of beer duty. The biggest Dublin brewer at the time was Sweetmans, who operated five breweries in the city.

Murphy's Cooperage

The popularity of porter prompted two Northern Protestants, William Beamish and William Crawford, to abandon their butter-and-beef business in Cork and go into brewing. They joined with two others who had been brewing ale, and created the Cork Porter

Brewery in 1792. By the early nineteenth century, Beamish and Crawford had become the biggest brewery in the then United Kingdom, selling 100,000 barrels a year, to Guinness's 66,000.

Irish brewers did not simply adopt porter, however, but were instrumental in developing one of the world's great beer styles – Irish dry stout. Following the introduction of a tax on malt in 1786, brewers began to mix unmalted barley into the grist, thus saving on duty. This unmalted barley was roasted, and gave the stout an uncompromising roasted bitterness and dryness, which remain the hallmarks of the style.

GUINNESS IN THE ASCENDANCY

The Great Famine in the mid-nineteenth century and the ensuing migration from the country resulted in many brewery closures and a huge loss in trade.

Before the Famine, there were more than a hundred breweries in operation, but by 1900 the number had dwindled to thirty-six. Although Beamish and Crawford did not close, they never regained their ascendancy in Ireland; by contrast, Guinness went from strength to strength, and by 1900 had become the biggest brewery in Europe.

Prior to 1850, the market for beer was limited to towns and cities, due to the countryside being essentially a subsistence economy with a taste for poitín – which had a higher alcohol content than beer, and was cheaper to make on a small scale. The big city brewers were chiefly making porter, due to the size of their market and the economies of scale associated with porter brewing, while the brewers in the small country towns generally concentrated on ales.

After 1850, although brewing remained a trade located in the towns and cities, the advent of the canals, followed by the railways, enabled

An early motorised dray leaves St James's Gate

breweries to distribute beyond their locale. Guinness were quick to take advantage of these new modes of transport, and this was one key to their success. The company established a network of agents throughout the country and contracted local bottlers to bottle Guinness. They created a national distribution network at a time when most other breweries concentrated on their locality.

Another key to Guinness's success was the quality of the beer. In 1821, Guinness decided to disregard the cost of raw materials and labour and instead to concentrate on the quality of their beer. Fresh casks were despatched from Dublin that would mature, or condition, en route, arriving ready to be bottled or drunk in the pub. By 1839, output at Guinness had gone up fourfold.

This striking growth continued throughout the nineteenth century, and by 1900 the run-down brewery that had been bought in 1759 was a giant, covering so much acreage in St James's Gate that it needed its own narrow-gauge railway system. It should also be said that Guinness had a third weapon in its arsenal: a taste for undercutting its rivals. Dublin brewers had in place a price agreement, but this was broken by Guinness on more than one occasion. Discounts were given to publicans: the brewery waged a price war which hit its profits but enabled it to gain market share. Many rivals found it difficult to compete and either closed, were bought up by Guinness, or found it easier to become bottlers for Guinness rather than continue to brew their own beer. Guinness was able to adopt this

approach because of the economies of scale it could generate from the vigorous export trade it had developed. By 1902, Guinness was available almost everywhere in Ireland.

The two big Cork brewers, Beamish and Crawford, and since 1856 Murphy's, kept Guinness at bay due to the tied-house system. In Cork and the locality, pubs were tied to taking only Beamish and Crawford or Murphy's products. This could be due to a variety of factors. For example, the brewery may have owned the pub itself and then be letting it to the publican on a long lease, or the brewery may have owned the licence but not the pub. Having an estate of tied houses meant a guaranteed market for the brewery's products and kept competitors at bay.

In Ulster, brewing was never as important an industry as it was elsewhere in Ireland. The biggest brewery was Thomas Caffrey's in west Belfast. Caffrey was an employee of the exotically named Clotworthy Dobbin, who established a brewery in 1820. Caffrey married one of Dobbin's daughters and built a larger brewery, named the Mountain Brewery, which opened in 1897.

One of the more interesting casualties in the brewing industry during this time was the short-lived Dartry Brewery in Dublin. Built on the banks of the Dodder, it was Ireland's first lager brewery, but lasted only five years, closing in 1897. Lager was little known in Ireland at the time and did not take off until the mid-twentieth century.

TOWARDS MONOPOLY

Ireland entered the twentieth century with thirty-six breweries but, tragically, three-quarters of these would be no more by 1970.

The two big Cork brewers had already bought and closed some small breweries in the City and County. However, the first crack in their own tied house system happened in 1920 when a six-week strike closed both breweries. This meant that they had to allow publicans to get their stout from elsewhere, and Guinness stepped in to fill the breach. Guinness had now established a foothold in Cork which it never completely relinquished. Competition was also eliminated in Kilkenny when Smithwick's bought and closed their rivals, the Sullivan's Brewery on James Street, in 1914.

Many breweries closed between the two world wars, especially during the 1920s. By 1939, more than half of the thirty-six were gone. In the newly created Northern Ireland, only Caffrey's remained, with the Enniskillen Brewery and McConnells of Belfast closing.

In the Irish Free State many local breweries closed, such as Murphy's of Clonmel – whose buildings were inherited by Bulmers Cider – Wickams of Wexford and Cassidy's of Monasterevin. Others, such as Foley's of Sligo and Egans of Tullamore, ceased brewing and became bottlers of Guinness; the latter's brewery tap is a popular pub in the town. The squeeze put on by Guinness was also felt in Dublin as its rivals closed, leaving Guinness and the Mountjoy Brewery of Russell Street as the remaining brewers in the city.

As World War II began, sixteen breweries remained on the island of Ireland. One of these was, remarkably, a new operation. The Regal Lager Brewery was founded by James Fitzsimmons in Kells, County Meath in 1937. He was originally a baker but had studied brewing in Munich. Unfortunately he was many years ahead of his time; brewing not just any old lager but, by all accounts, a pilsner and a bock. Regal Lager closed in the early 1950s and Fitzsimmons predicted that a lager brewery would be built soon by a brewer with more resources. Only a few years later lager began to make its first serious inroads into the stout market in Ireland and Harp Lager would become an established brand.

The development of porter had a lasting impact on Irish brewing but, interestingly, the next big revolution in the beer world – pale ale – did not. In

Great Britain, tastes were changing and porter was in slow decline in the face of pale ale. Pale ale came about as a result of the ability of maltsters to use coke to lightly kiln their malt. Pale ale was and is a bright chestnut-coloured beer that visibly sparkled in the glass. Porter brewing went into freefall during the First World War when the use of coke was restricted, making it difficult to produce the dark malts used for porter. These restrictions were not implemented in Ireland, no doubt due to the volatile political situation at the time. This meant that stout remained the drink of choice.

GLOBAL INTERESTS AND GUINNESS DOMINANCE

Although breweries were closing, thirteen remained, and a degree of loyalty to the local brewer helped keep many afloat until the early 1950s.

Most local brewers lacked the capacity to expand however and could not compete with the substantial economies of scale of a major player such as Guinness. Smithwick's in Kilkenny were very aware of this problem and began to expand to gain a national identity with their ale. As part of this expansion they bought the Great Northern Brewery in Dundalk in 1953, but subsequently leased it to a Guinness-led consortium in 1957.

The real path towards monopolisation began in 1952 when Guinness bought Cherry's Creywell Brewery in New Ross. There were very good reasons for doing so: an Act passed by Dáil Éireann in 1951 required companies trading in the Republic of Ireland to be registered there. Guinness had been registered in London since 1886 and needed a Brewers for Sale licence to operate in the Republic. A second reason was that Ind Coope, a big brewer from Burton-on-Trent, had a large stake in Dundalk's Macardle Moore Brewery and were getting their keg ale Double Diamond into the Irish market. Cherry's was an ale brewery and gave Guinness a way into the developing ale market. As a result of this purchase, Guinness became involved in ale brewing again for the first time in more than 150 years.

Under Guinness, Cherry's merged with Drogheda's Cairnes brewery to create the Cherry-Cairnes Group and for a while successfully marketed Phoenix Ale. The Creywell brewery was closed in 1954 as it did not have sufficient capacity to meet demand. Brewing was

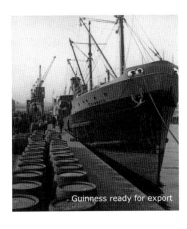

Guinness ready for export

transferred to the old Davis-Strangman brewery in Waterford, which had been mothballed since 1948. Cairnes brewery fell victim to rationalisation in 1959, when all production was concentrated at Waterford, leading to the dissolving of the Cherry-Cairnes partnership.

Other casualties during the 1950s were Guinness's last remaining rivals in Dublin, the Mountjoy Brewery, which closed in 1957. Also George Killian Lett's of Enniscorthy, who only ever had a local market, found it hard to compete with the national brands. Lett's were, however, interesting from a brewing point of view having Ireland's only set of Burton Unions – a special system of fermentation pioneered in Burton-on-Trent. Curiously the Lett's name lives on as the company licensed its name to Coors in the US, who market it as 'Killians Irish Red', and Pelforth in France (part of the Heineken Group), where it is known as 'George Killian Biere Rousse'.

The Guinness-led consortium which had been leasing Dundalk's Great Northern Brewery from Smithwick's, acquired it in 1960 and built the Harp Lager Brewery on the site. The brewing of Harp Lager began there in 1961. Also in 1961, 'Irish Ale Breweries' was created when Cherry's, owned by Guinness, merged with Macardle Moore, substantially owned by England's Allied Breweries, Ind Coope's successors. Guinness had a two-thirds share in Irish Ale Breweries to Allied's one-third.

In 1965 Smithwicks joined Irish Ale Breweries and, tragically, the last independent brewer, Perry's of Rathdowney, County Laois were bought by Irish Ale Breweries and shut down in 1967.

The two Cork brewers were also feeling the pinch. Beamish and Crawford were taken over by Canadian Breweries in 1962, beating a bid from Guinness, who also had an approach to Murphy's rebuffed around this time. Later in the 1960s, Murphy's was taken over by English company Watney-Mann, brewers of Red Barrel.

In Northern Ireland brewing at Caffrey's Mountain Brewery had ceased in 1950. In 1952 it was purchased by a consortium of Ulster Vintners and renamed the Ulster Brewery. In the mid-1960s it was taken over by Anglo-Scottish concern United Brewers, who would later become Tennents-Bass.

The other major development in the 1960s was the introduction of draught stout, a kegged beer with a large proportion of nitrogen in the keg and a dispensing system that creates a creamy head. Before this, stout in larger pubs situated in cities and big towns was a blended beer known as 'high cask-low cask'. Two-thirds of a pint was drawn by handpump from the high cask, which contained a fresh stout that would be highly conditioned. Once the head subsided, the remaining third was drawn from the low cask, which contained old, flat, somewhat stale beer full of character. Getting the right mix was the sign of a good barman. By contrast, in smaller, often countryside pubs, beer would come from one fresh barrel, and be poured into a jug and then into a glass to reduce its fizziness. Draught stout replaced both of these cask-conditioned stouts, but the ritual of the two-stage pour remains, despite the beer coming from a single keg. Draught stout also put an end to publicans having to bottle their own stout in-house which was not a favourite part of the job.

By the end of the 1970s there were eight breweries remaining. Five were owned, or at least controlled, by Guinness. Tennents-Bass and Canadian Breweries owned a brewery each whilst Watney-Mann had pulled out of Murphy's, leaving the brewery in the hands of Taiscí Stáit Teoranta, the state rescue service.

The other significant development in the 1980s was the ending of the tied-house system in Cork. In the late 1960s, Beamish and Crawford had relaunched their stout under the moniker 'Tower', but this had proved unsuccessful. Their owners decided to concentrate on Carling Black Label and Bass Ale. This, together with pressure from their tenants, led to the decision to allow their publicans to sell Guinness. Murphy's resisted the tenants' demands but began to sell some of the tied houses in the early 1970s due to the cost of their upkeep. When Murphy's went into receivership in 1982, the remainder of the pubs were sold to make ends meet.

Irish Ale Breweries was dissolved in 1988, with all the breweries becoming part of Guinness Ireland. Similarly, the Guinness-led consortium that owned the Harp Lager Brewery unravelled, and the brewery passed into Guinness ownership. Guinness, including Guinness Ireland, and Grand Met merged in 1997 to form the large multinational Diageo, whose head offices are in London. Brewing continues at three sites: St James's Gate in Dublin, Smithwick's in Kilkenny, and the now-renamed Great Northern Brewery in Dundalk. Macardle Moore, Dundalk's other brewery, was shut down by Diageo in 2001, whilst brewing ceased in Waterford in 2003. The Waterford brewery still exists and is now used to make Guinness Extract, a dried hopped wort that is used by Guinness breweries throughout the world.

Beamish and Crawford changed hands again taken in 1987 when Elders IXL, who would become the Foster's Group, took over Canadian Breweries. Ownership changed yet again in 1995 as they became part of Scottish Courage, the brewing division of Scottish & Newcastle. Murphy's went into receivership in 1982 and were bought by Heineken a year later. Caffrey's Irish Ale, brewed in Belfast, was a runaway success for Tennents-Bass in the mid-1990s but it disappeared as quickly as it had arrived. Tennents-Bass subsequently became part of Belgian giant Interbrew, latterly named InBev, who closed down the Belfast brewery in 2005.

The drinking preferences of the Irish public have also changed markedly in the last forty years. In the 1960s, stout made up three-quarters of the market. By the 1980s, this had dropped to two-thirds. In Ireland, stout has proved remarkably resilient in the face of lager, but lager finally outstripped stout in 1999. Stout currently accounts for around 40 percent of the market, lager 52 percent, and ale just 5 percent.

CRAFT BREWING ARRIVES

Ireland was one of the last major brewing nations to experience a boom among craft brewers.

There is no doubt that the near-monopoly position of Guinness in the Republic and the Guinness/Tennents-Bass duopoly in Northern Ireland played a role in making it difficult for small brewers to find a route to market, especially in pubs.

However, after a few faltering steps, craft brewing has arrived providing

much needed choice for the Irish drinker.

Initial attempts at establishing craft brewing in the early 1980s unfortunately failed. Dempsey's of Inchicore and Harty's of Blessington lasted a very short time. Interestingly, Liam LaHart was behind

Harty's and Oliver Hughes was involved in both initiatives, these men would later found the Porterhouse. These were primarily cask-conditioned ale breweries, but the Irish market proved very difficult for a type of beer that had did not have the same tradition as it does in Britain.

In Northern Ireland, the Herald Brewery in Coleraine lasted four years before closing in 1987 and the Maiden Oak, later Foyle, brewery in Derry/Londonderry lasted a similar time from 1985. However, one real-ale brewer thankfully survived – the Hilden Brewery just outside Belfast started in 1981 and is still going to this day. The stronger British influence in Northern Ireland makes selling cask-conditioned ale here somewhat less difficult than in the Republic but, nevertheless, it is still a challenge in a market effectively controlled by a duopoly.

The first wave of craft brewers began in 1995 with Biddy Early in County Clare. Others followed and by the late 1990s Ireland had around fourteen craft brewers. This gave Ireland its largest number of breweries since before the Second World War. However only just over half survived. Gone are the Irish Brewing Company in Newbridge, Dwans in Thurles, Balbriggan Brewery and the Dublin Brewing Company of Smithfield who did enjoy some initial success with brands such as Revolution Red, D'Arcy's Stout, Becket's Lager and Maeve's Crystal Beer. The Emerald brewery in Roscommon is now brewing again having changed hands, and will be the (possibly temporary) home of the

Hooker brewery.

This wave almost exclusively copied the large brewers against whom they were competing in that, virtually to a brewer, each one produced a stout, a red ale and a lager. They accepted drinkers' preferences rather than challenging them. In reflection, many admit that this may have been a mistake. Taking on big brewers' brands, backed as they are by massive marketing budgets, is tough and many craft breweries failed because of this. Others were speculators, believing that craft beer was about to take-off in Ireland and there was money to be made. The main problem they encountered was that the Irish drinker tended to be very brand loyal so that getting someone to change from Guinness to a mysterious new stout was very difficult indeed.

Times and tastes are changing however and, as the Celtic Tiger roars, imported beers are slowly becoming more readily available, challenging the stout/lager/red ale troika and the established brands as well. People are also experimenting more when it comes to their choice of beer. This combination of factors is changing the face of the Irish brewing industry. A key development has been the achievement of an excise-duty rebate for small brewers. A similar system was already in place in the UK a few years earlier but was finally achieved in the Republic in 2004. Irish craft brewers campaigned long and hard for this and were supported by noted Trinity College economist, Constantin Gurdgiev. Now, brewers whose output is less than 20,000 hectolitres a year are entitled to a 50 percent rebate on excise duty. This benefits small brewers and has been a great help in increasing choice for consumers.

Thanks to the introduction of the excise-duty rebate, a second wave of craft brewing is beginning to rise, with some getting their beer brewed elsewhere to see how it sells before committing the required capital for a brewery in Ireland. Moreover, the influx of imported beers has opened people up to new tastes, making it possible for craft brewers to brew niche beers distinct from those of the big brewers. The brewers of the second wave and a few of the first wave are doing just that.

The second wave is only just beginning and there are two new breweries – one in Clifden, County Galway, and the other in Ramelton, County Donegal – that may well be on-stream in the very near future. With more interest than ever in quality local produce and people becoming more experimental in their drinking, the time may be ripe for the small-scale Irish craft brewers to supply their local markets in the way that the long-forgotten small brewers of Ireland once did.

BREWING BEER

Although beer is inextricably linked to brewing, this is actually only one small part of the process of turning a crop, mainly barley, into a refreshing drink of moderate alcoholic strength.

Because beer is an everyday drink people often assume it is easy to make. On the contrary, it takes considerable skill at each stage of production. Wine is in essence a simple product – you crush the grape to get its juice that contains the sugars on which the yeast will feed to produce alcohol. Wine is basically alcoholic fruit juice. But if you crush barley you won't get any sugar, there's a bit more to making beer.

INGREDIENTS

Beer is a product of the land, connected to our agricultural past. It is a natural drink made from four key ingredients – malted barley, water, hops and yeast – each of which will contribute something to the flavour of the finished product.

Malted Barley

All beer in Ireland starts in a golden field of barley, a cereal crop that thrives in northern latitudes where grapes do not.

Like grapes, it comes in many different varieties with wonderful names such as Maris Otter – the Rolls-Royce of barleys – Golden Promise, Halcyon and Pipkin to name but a few.

As it is one of the most characterful cereals, barley is the traditional brewing grain imparting clean, sweetish and biscuity flavours. Crucially for the early brewers, it also has a husk that acts as a natural filter during the mashing stage of brewing.

Wheat beers, as the name implies, are made from wheat but, despite the name, always contain at least 50 percent barley. Wheat imparts tarter, fruitier flavours compared to other grains but does not have a husk and therefore, on its own, clogs up brewing vessels. This is why even in wheat beers, barley still plays a key role.

Making an alcoholic drink from barley is not straightforward, as barley contains only starch, whereas sugar is needed to make alcohol. The trick is to turn this starch into sugar for the yeast to feed upon to create alcohol. It takes two steps to achieve this transformation. The first step takes place at a maltings, usually separate from any brewery these days; the second step takes place at the brewery itself.

barley with a shovel to let it breathe. Such floor maltings, as they are known, are labour intensive and are now few and far between. Most modern maltings accomplish this in a rotating drum.

Left in this state, the germinating grain would begin to consume the starch needed by the brewer. The sign that the starch is unlocked is the appearance of rootlets breaking through the husk – the grain is

Barley

At the maltings the starch is unlocked, a process known as 'modification'. The barley arrives at the maltings and is firstly steeped in water. After absorbing the moisture, it is then left to dry and begins to germinate – as the barley grain is, of course, a potential barley plant. Starting germination unlocks the starch as the embryonic barley plant will need its starch as fuel to grow.

Traditionally, this part of the malting process was done by spreading the barley over a floor. The maltster would regularly turn the

beginning to germinate and is now known as 'green malt'. Once this happens, the germination has to be arrested, effectively killing the embryonic barley plant, and thus providing the brewer with the starch needed to make beer. Kilning was the traditional method to arrest germination and was done by spreading the green malt over a heated floor. In industrial maltings, the green malt is placed in an externally heated drum. Initially, the heat is gentle to arrest germination. The heat will then be increased to the required specification. The hotter the kilning, the darker the malt.

At the end of this process the barley grain is now edible malt. Although it looks like raw barley, it has been radically altered: a barley grain is rock hard whereas malt can be bitten into and is biscuit-sweet to the taste.

The two main maltsters in Ireland are Minch Norton at Athy in County Kildare and the Malting Company of Ireland in Cork. However, they only really do pale malt so any brewery needing speciality malts have to source them from English maltsters.

There are many types of malt, the difference between them being the degree to which they have been kilned. Each gives a different colour and character to the final beer. Brewers will select their malt carefully, depending on the type of beer they are brewing and what they are trying to achieve in terms of colour and flavour.

The main malt in lager is known as pilsner or lager malt. This is lightly kilned and therefore imparts little colour to the final beer, which will be wonderfully bright and golden. The base malt for ale is pale malt. This is

kilned slightly longer and imparts a slightly deeper amber colour to the final beer.

There are also many other speciality malts. Chocolate malt is kilned at a high temperature until the grains are dark brown and look like coffee beans. The main role of chocolate malt is to add colour as well as a delicious chocolate and coffee character to stouts and porters. Black malt is kilned at a higher temperature again and is burned to carbonisation, giving an espresso-like bitterness to dark beers.

Crystal malt and caramalt are stewed malts. After germination the green malt is heated in a sealed kiln preventing the moisture from escaping. Some of the starch converts into sugar, the vents in the kiln are then opened and the sugar crystallises. Much of this sugar cannot be converted into alcohol by brewer's yeast and therefore it remains in the final beer giving it a nutty flavour and full palate.

Roasted barley is not malted but simply roasted until black. It contains no starch for the brewer, so its function is to provide a roasted, dry aroma and flavour and is popular in stout, especially the Irish style. It also helps the finished beer retain a good head of foam.

Finally, there is wheat malt. Used mainly in wheat beer, but small amounts can also used by ale brewers to help maintain a head of foam on the finished beer.

Minch Norton Maltings, Athy

There are other ingredients used in some beers and these are collectively known as 'adjuncts'. The main adjuncts are unmalted grains such as rice or corn, wheat flour, flaked grains, torrefied grain (scorched and similar to popcorn) and brewing sugar. Many craft brewers either use very small quantities of adjuncts or, more often, none at all. When they are used, they have specific tasks, such as to aid head retention, help clarify the beer, and assist the brewer in achieving the correct flavour and colour balance. Large-scale brewers often dilute their beer, especially lager, with large quantities of adjuncts. This is often done to save costs but the use of too many adjuncts can result in losing the flavour imparted by the barley and the beer will be bland and characterless.

Water
Beer is mainly water, for example, a beer of 5 percent alcohol will be 95 percent water.

Unsurprisingly, brewers take great care of their water supply. In a brewery water is used for a number of tasks, such as cleaning, but the water used for brewing gets special treatment and even a special name – 'brewing liquor', or 'liquor' for short – the quality of which has always been a major concern for brewers. Testament to this is the fact that in the past, when the quality of the local water supply was unreliable, people would drink beer for refreshment and to quench their thirst as the brewing process renders the water safe to drink.

The crucial consideration for the brewer is the water's relative hardness or softness. All rainwater is slightly acidic and if it falls on soft rock, such as limestone, it will dissolve the mineral salts in the rock. This will render the final water 'hard' as it contains all those dissolved salts. On the other hand, rainwater falling on hard rock, such as granite, will be low in mineral salts and therefore produces what is commonly called 'soft' water.

Burton-on-Trent in England became one of the world's major brewing centres in the nineteenth century due to the quality of its water. The local water contained a huge concentration of salts that made it perfect for brewing pale ale. Other brewers clambered to open breweries in Burton until the industrial revolution made it possible to replicate the water by adding the requisite salts, a technique still known today as 'burtonisation'. These days many brewers will filter their water to rid it of impurities such as nitrates from agriculture, then burtonise as required.

Hop bines

Whereas hard water makes the best ale, stouts and lagers are traditionally best brewed from soft water, which is found in the traditional centres of stout and porter brewing – Dublin and London – and in the lager brewing centres around Plzen in the Czech Republic.

The key salts for brewing are gypsum (calcium sulphate), which is good for mashing and assists the releasing of aromas and flavours from the hops, and Epsom salts (magnesium sulphate), which aids the yeast in its work of making alcohol. All brewers will want some of these salts in their liquor so each will burtonise to some degree. The final effect of the water on the finished products will be noticed primarily in the feel of the beer in the mouth. Lager and stout made with soft water will have a smooth texture whereas ales made with hard water will have a certain 'bite'.

Hops
The hop plant is a member of the hemp family and a close cousin of cannabis.

To flourish it requires dry, sandy soil and long hours of sunshine. Hops, which impart bitterness, flavour and preservative qualities, are a vital component in the vast majority of beer available today. However, this was not always the case, especially in Ireland.

Until the 1500s the main drink in the British Isles was 'ale', a strong, heavy brew of malted barley and water. This was an exceptionally sweet drink and was usually flavoured with herbs and spices such as bog myrtle, yarrow and rosemary to counteract this sweetness. During the 1500s 'beer' arrived in England from the continent and caused great controversy. 'Beer' was hopped and seen as an inferior foreign product to the domestic ale. However, by the late sixteenth century beer had swept all

Hob Cone

before it and hops were beginning to be cultivated in southern England.

Irish ale, however, remained

unhopped until the 1700s. This was due to the unsuitable climate as well as a high export tax on hops from England.

Commercial hop growers train the plant to climb poles, or bines. The flowers, or cones, develop and reach maturity by late August and into September when they are harvested. The traditional hand picking has now been replaced by mechanised harvesting.

Hop cones will rot quickly so they must be dried within hours of being picked. Traditionally this was done in oasthouses where the hops were spread over perforated floors and circulated with warm air. Nowadays they are put on a conveyor and go through a drier. Once dried, they are put into sacks called 'hop pockets' and can last for up to two years.

Many breweries are now geared for pelletised hops rather than whole cones. To produce pellets, the cones are milled, compacted and then vacuum-packed. Big brewers often use 'hop extract'; a thick, syrupy, jelly-like substance made from crushing and boiling the hops. Many craft brewers would frown on such a process as it can give the finished beer a somewhat harsh taste.

The hop cone has oils, which provide the aroma and flavour of the final beer; alpha acids, which impart bitterness; and beta acids, that work with the tannin in the hops to ward off infection. Hops come in two basic types: those with high acid, called

'bittering hops', are used for, unsurprisingly, imparting bitterness in the final beer; and hops with low acid for aroma and flavour – 'aroma hops'.

Wine grapes such as Pinot Noir, Cabernet Sauvignon and Merlot give the finished wine its distinctiveness. Similarly, the hop variety or varieties used will give the beer its distinctive aroma and flavour. Malted barley also contributes to flavour and the job of the brewer is to use hops to balance the sweetness of the malt.

Germany is the biggest hop-producing nation, with varieties such as Hallertauer Mittelfrüh, Hersbrucker, Tettnang and Perle typically providing a 'noble' aroma and delicate bitterness. Germany is closely followed by the United States, with Willamette, Mount Hood, Chinook, Cascade and Galena among the American hop varieties. These often provide a distinctive citrussy quality to the beer. There is a discernable trend in the US craft beer movement towards 'extreme beers', highly hopped beers with strong flavour and robust bitterness.

The Czech Saaz or Zatec hop is very much sought after for lager brewing and is a must for any authentic pilsner. It provides a delicate but noticeable bitterness and a superb flowery aroma. English hop varieties, such as Goldings and Fuggles, named after the farmers that originally propagated them, often provide a spicy quality and have been

Kent oasthouse

joined by other varieties such as Brewers Gold, Target, Progress, Northdown and Challenger.

Irish brewers use hops from all over the world, as the wet Irish climate makes hop growing difficult. Although the hops come from all over the world, Irish breweries tend to source them from English hop merchants. Not all beer is hopped and there are some that still use spices and herbs as flavouring today, echoing past traditions. In Ireland, the Biddy Early Brewery in County Clare uses the traditional herb bog myrtle, grown locally, to flavour its Red Biddy ale. In Scotland, heather, pine sprigs, and even seaweed are used as flavouring and while the famous Belgian wheat beer Hoegaarden is flavoured with orange peel and coriander.

Yeast
Without yeast, beer would have no alcohol.

Before the late 1800s the role of yeast was not understood and the process of turning a sweet liquid brew into ale or beer was seen as mystical or religious and given the term 'godisgood'. Brewers learnt, however, that by skimming the head of foam off a fermenting brew and adding it to a fresh brew, the same process would happen again.

The mysteries of yeast were revealed by the work of Dutch scientist Anton van Leeuwenhoek and later by Louis Pasteur. They discovered that godisgood was actually a living creature, a single celled fungus to be precise. This fungus eats the sugar in the brew and reproduces, creating equal amounts of carbon dioxide and alcohol.

Before this work brewers were unaware that, as the brew cooled, wild yeasts would attack the liquid. Wild yeasts are indisciplined and inefficient and only partly convert the sugar into alcohol. They also leave behind a large quantity of esters, which give the beer fruity flavours. Further storage after fermentation would develop a sourness, due to the work of lactic acid bacteria. Some beer is still made by this method today. In Belgium, Lambic beer is made by spontaneous wild yeast fermentation and is a very complex product, if somewhat challenging to drink in its raw form or as 'gueuze' (blended with older brews). Fruit such as cherry and raspberry are added to make it more palatable. In much of Africa, many native brewers brew another challenging drink: a porridge-like beer called Chibuku, which is made from sorghum and fermented by wild yeast.

The work of van Leeuwenhoek and Pasteur showed that yeast is

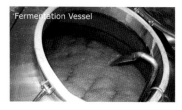

Fermentation Vessel

made up of several competing strains, and by skimming the yeast from the top of a fermenting brew brewers were, unknowingly, beginning the process of selecting the best strains for brewing. Yeast was beginning to be disciplined.

Once the mystery of yeast was revealed, brewers began the process of selecting the strains they wanted to create their own yeast cultures. They did this by removing unnecessary strains that were slowing the fermentation process.

There are now two main types of brewer's yeast: ale and lager. All beer, except those made by spontaneous wild yeast fermentation, are either ales or lagers, depending on which type of brewers yeast is being used. Ale yeasts work in a temperate environment, anything from around 12°C, though this rises as the yeast gets to work. Ale fermentation is

traditionally carried out in open-topped vessels, and during fermentation the yeast rises to the top, creating a thick head of foam which protects the brew from infection. This head would be collected and stored to start the next fermentation. Many ale brewers these days use closed conical fermenters in which the yeast gradually falls to the bottom and can be conveniently collected for storage and further use.

Although many ale brewers have now cultured their yeast down to one or two strains, ale yeasts are not wholly efficient in that they leave behind certain sugars and esters, giving ales a fruity complexity. As well as what is usually understood as ale, true stouts are also made with an ale yeast and so are wheat beers, therefore both are members of the ale family.

The word lager comes from the German word Lagerung, meaning to store. German brewers found out that storing beer in icy caves during the hot summer months kept it from becoming infected. What was actually happening was that the cold kept wild yeast and bacteria dormant. In 1883, Emil Christian Hansen, a brewing scientist at Carlsberg in Copenhagen, found out that certain strains of Bavarian yeast work at low temperatures during the storage time. His work in selecting down to a single strain of yeast that can work at low temperatures is the basis for today's lager yeast.

Barley germinating at the maltings

Lager yeast works at a lower temperature than ale yeast, around 5°C. Because of this lower temperature, the yeast works more slowly than ale yeast and can take up to two weeks to ferment a brew – about twice the length of an ale yeast fermentation. The resulting beer will then need to be stored – lagered – at close to 0°C, where the remaining yeast will slowly eat away at the remaining sugars turning them into alcohol and carbon dioxide. Good Czech and German pilsners will receive months of lagering, creating a clean and rounded final beer, but many of the major lager brands get as little as two weeks resulting in an inferior product with an inappropriate sweetness.

As it is a pure culture, lager yeast is very efficient and converts almost all of the sugars before falling to the bottom of the vessel from where it can be collected. A good lagering time results in a clean, crisp and dry beer that is very refreshing, though less complex than ale.

Few brewers now skim the yeast from one brew to start the next. They are more likely to use dried yeast, which is collected from the brew, dried, pressed, then refrigerated until required.

Cleanliness is paramount at a brewery in case the yeast gets infected. If this happens, the brew will have to be dumped and the plant sterilised. Brewers are loath to change their yeast strain as it develops its own characteristics over time and contributes to the overall flavour of the beer. Samples of yeast will be lodged at a yeast bank in case of infection so the brewer can draw on a supply of the original. After a few generations, a new yeast culture will be propagated from the original source even if no infection has occurred.

BREWING
At the brewery, these ingredients will be put together to create the desired beer.

Although different beers will be brewed in diverse ways, each beer has to go through four stages at the brewery: mashing, brewing, fermentation and conditioning.

Mashing
The first stage is called 'mashing'. Malted barley arrives at the brewery and is ground into a rough flour known as 'grist'.

This will be mixed with hot brewing liquor just prior to entering the mash tun – a round vessel with rotating blades which stir the mixture. In here 'conversion' takes place, as the starch in the malt transforms into sugar.

There are different ways to mash but the common way in Ireland is called an 'infusion mash'. Here the grist is mixed with hot liquor at around 65°C and the mixture will remain in the mash tun for one to two hours. Some brewers may use a 'step mash', where the temperature of the mixture in the mash tun is raised in a series of steps.

The temperature is crucial as it is in the mash tun that enzymes in the malt go to work and convert the starch into sugar, which then dissolves into the liquor. If the temperature is too hot the enzymes will be destroyed; too cold and much of the starch will remain unconverted.

Once the brewer judges the mash to be complete, the bottom of the tun is opened, revealing a perforated base which filters the husks of grain from the liquid. Perforated tubes then rotate, spraying the grains with hot water to flush out any remaining sugar, a procedure known as 'sparging'. The sweet liquid that emerges from mashing is called 'wort' (pronounced 'wurt'). The spent grains that remain are often sold to farmers as cattle feed.

In some breweries this process will be divided between two vessels. Conversion will take place in the mash tun but the mash will then be pumped into another vessel, a lauter tun, for clarifying the wort. This speeds up the process: as one wort is being clarified, another mash can start.

The wort then goes to a receiving vessel in preparation for being pumped to the brew-kettle for the next stage: brewing.

Brewing
In the brew-kettle the wort is boiled and it is here that hops are added.

Boiling sterilises the wort and the hops themselves also act as a preservative. Brewing normally lasts around ninety minutes and there may be a number of hop additions, depending on what the brewer wants to achieve. Hops added at the beginning of the boil – 'kettle hops' – are for bitterness, as boiling results in the extraction of alpha acids whilst any aroma or flavour will evaporate. Hops added towards the end – 'late

hops' – give the finished beer the desired aroma and flavour.

Brewing sugar may also be added into the copper to increase the fermentable material as well as to add colour and flavour. The hopped wort will then be clarified to remove the hops and any 'trub' – residue containing proteins and other matter. This is often done by putting the hopped wort through a whirlpool in the base of the brew-kettle, and then cooled to around 18°C for ale and around 5°C for lager.

Fermentation
The hopped wort is then ready for fermentation.

Traditionally ales would have been fermented in large open vessels with the head of foam from the activity of the yeast keeping the brew safe from infection. These days many brewers use closed conicals, cylindrical tanks with a cone shaped base, vessels that were more commonly found in lager brewing.

Yeast will be pitched into the hopped wort already residing in the fermentation vessel and the process of making alcohol begins. Ale fermentation tends to be quick and lively and may last less than seven days. The temperature will increase as the yeast gets to work and the process also creates 'esters'; chemical compounds giving fruity aromas to the final beer. The fermenter must be cooled to prevent the temperature rising too much, otherwise the yeast will become sluggish. Lager fermentation takes longer, around two weeks, and the purity of the yeast strain creates very few esters. Again the temperature will need to be controlled to prevent the development of off-flavours.

Eventually the yeast is overcome by the alcohol and begins to clump together. In closed conicals the yeast falls to the bottom, where it can be collected. What comes out is termed 'green beer', beer that is not yet quite ready to drink. This is collected from a tap some way up the cone above the level at which the yeast has settled.

Conditioning
The green beer will be 'racked' from the fermenting vessel to a conditioning tank as it will need a period of conditioning to purge itself of the rougher alcohols.

Ales only take a few days conditioning. After that they will usually be filtered to remove any remaining yeast or other haze and may be pasteurised. They will then be carbonated, by injecting a 50:50 mix of carbon dioxide and nitrogen, to create a sparkle, and be put into a sealed keg or bottle. Pasteurisation, though, often removes some of the flavours of the final beer, as does nitrogenation – a way of getting a smooth beer with a dense, creamy head.

Some ales will be cask-conditioned. These will not be conditioned in the brewery. The green beer is racked into casks, with some yeast, straight from the fermenter, without filtration or pasteurisation. They leave the brewery unfinished and complete their conditioning in the pub cellar, due to the presence of the yeast. To achieve a bright product they will usually have isinglass finings added, made from the swim bladder of the sturgeon, and this will slowly attract yeast particles to the bottom of the cask. A small natural sparkle will develop during cask conditioning and such beers will not need to be artificially carbonated.

A few bottled beers are treated in a similar way by bottling with some yeast. Such beers are bottle-conditioned and will have a natural carbonation due to the action of the yeast in the bottle. These beers need to be poured carefully if a bright product is desired, so that the yeast does not make its way into the glass and cloud the beer.

Lager is usually racked into lagering tanks where the yeast continues to work slowly through the remaining sugar until it falls to the bottom. The temperature will be close to 0°C and the process can take anything from a few weeks to months for the best Czech and German pilsners. Early on, the tanks are left open so that rough alcohols escape with the carbon dioxide. They are then sealed so that carbon dioxide builds up in the beer. The finished product will then be filtered and often pasteurised and the carbonation adjusted, usually by injecting carbon dioxide into the keg, can or bottle.

Nearly all stouts and some ales available on draught in Ireland are nitrogenated so that the customer gets a beer with a smooth mouthfeel and a thick, lasting, creamy head. To achieve this, the proportion of nitrogen in the gas mixture is increased to around 75:25, and the beer is dispensed using a special tap that forces it out under pressure.

Nitrogen bubbles are tiny compared to those of carbon dioxide and are not soluble in water so that once the beer is poured, the bubbles break out and form a stable head. The head is stable because nitrogen makes up 79 percent of the atmosphere and there is little difference between the concentration in the atmosphere and that in the head, so there is less incentive for the nitrogen to dissipate. The head on a conventionally carbonated beer does not last as long, being made up of a good percentage of carbon dioxide bubbles. As the concentration of carbon dioxide in the head is greater than that in the atmosphere the bubbles will eventually dissipate.

Nitrogenated beer is also available

canned and bottled, usually by inserting a 'widget', a small capsule, into the can or bottle to mimic the special beer tap and force the beer out at pressure, creating the thick creamy head.

MAIN BEER STYLES IN IRELAND

The types of beer brewed in Ireland are expanding as small brewers are becoming increasingly experimental. Three styles dominate, though two others are increasingly making their presence felt in Ireland of late.

Stout and Porter

For a style of beer synonymous with Ireland, it may be surprising that porter's origins lie in early-eighteenth-century London. Porter brewing was one of the major changes in brewing since the introduction of hops. Porter replaced a drink known as 'three threads' which was a blend of three types of beer. In the days of three threads, asking for a beer meant that the publican would draw measures from three casks to fill your tankard. The name 'porter' – it was originally called 'entire butt' – came about later due to the popularity of the beer among London's market porters. The strongest versions were known as 'stout porter', eventually becoming simply 'stout'.

The flood of porter into Ireland stimulated local breweries such as Beamish and Crawford in Cork and Guinness in Dublin to switch from ale to porter brewing. A duty on malt led them to mix some unmalted – and therefore untaxed – roasted barley into the grist, making it a drier drink and creating the style known as Irish Dry Stout.

Almost black in colour, the characteristics of the style are a great roasty aroma often mixed with hints of coffee and bitter chocolate. There is usually a good level of bitterness and a tang in the finish.

Porter tends to be lighter in body than dry stout and can be fruitier.

Irish Red Ale

Harking back to life before the dominance of stout is Irish Red Ale. Before hops became readily available, more localised herbs would have been used to flavour the beer. As hops were a late entrant into Irish brewing, this style of ale remains sweeter than its English counterparts.

A reddish-amber colour with an accent towards the sweetish malt rather than hops is the hallmark. Hints of toffee can also be found in some examples, as can some light fruitiness.

Lager and Pilsner

More than any other style of beer, it is lager that has swept all before it. Originally, lagers were dark brown brews – some still are – and hailed from Munich. However, it was in Plzen, in what is now the Czech Republic, that a golden lager was first brewed.

Before the 1840s, the colour of beer was not an issue as drinking vessels were opaque, being made from leather, wood, or metal. However, with the arrival of mass produced glass, the colour of beer took on a new importance. Also, the advent of the industrial revolution meant that malt could be kilned to a very light colour, creating a final product that looked bright and stunning in the new glassware.

Success bred imitations as the new style swept through Europe and went global as emigrants from the old countries travelled to the new world. A true lager, or pilsner, will have a good floral or grassy hop bouquet, possibly with hints of citrus and a refreshing dry bitter finish. Mass-produced lagers can be pale imitations of the real thing, lacking the bitterness and often having an inappropriate sweetness.

Bitter and Pale Ale

Bitter and pale ale are English styles and, in a similar way to lager, are both connected with new kilning methods and the mass production of glassware that came with the Industrial Revolution.

More of a chestnut colour than golden, they also visibly sparkle in glass in contrast to the cloudy brown ales that were previously popular. Bitter is slightly darker than pale ale and is very diverse in style but can exhibit nutty, spicy, peppery and fruity characteristics with a good bitter dryness in the finish. Pale ale often has citric and floral notes, again with a refreshing and moreish bitter finish.

Wheat Beer

There are two main kinds of wheat beer popular in Ireland – the south German and Belgian styles.

A key hallmark of the style is low hopping. The south German style was originally the preserve of the Bavarian royal family, who eventually allowed commercial brewers to make it for the masses. It usually comes filtered – Kristall – or unfiltered – Hefe (Hefe being the German for yeast).

This is a very refreshing style of beer with little bitterness due to the low hopping. The unfiltered version will be cloudy; have aromas reminiscent of banana, apples and cloves; and have a quenching tart finish, courtesy of the wheat. The filtered style loses some of the fruitiness but is cleaner tasting.

The Belgian style is often spiced with coriander and orange peel. It is also hazy, tart and refreshing, with citrus and coriander evident.

Breweries, Cidermakers and Pubs Specialising in Beer in Ireland

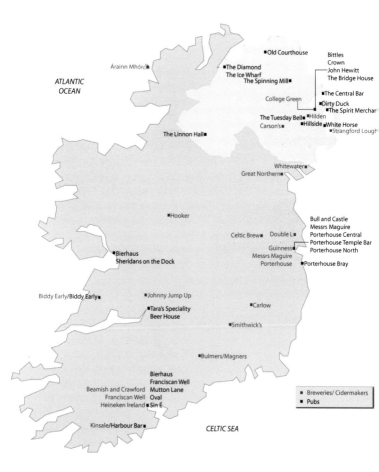

ATLANTIC OCEAN

Árainn Mhór■

■Old Courthouse

■The Diamond
The Ice Wharf
The Spinning Mill■

College Green

The Tuesday Bell■ ■Hilden
Carson's■ ■Hillside

Bittles
Crown
John Hewitt
The Bridge House

■The Central Bar

■Dirty Duck
■The Spirit Merchan

■White Horse
■Strangford Lough

The Linnon Hall■

Whitewater■
Great Northern■

■Hooker

Celtic Brew■ Double L■

Bull and Castle
Messrs Maguire
Porterhouse Central
Porterhouse Temple Bar
Porterhouse North

■Bierhaus
Sheridans on the Dock

Guinness■
Messrs Maguire
Porterhouse ■Porterhouse Bray

Biddy Early/Biddy Early■

■Johnny Jump Up

■Tara's Speciality
Beer House

■Carlow

■Smithwick's

■Bulmers/Magners

Bierhaus
Franciscan Well
Beamish and Crawford Mutton Lane
Franciscan Well Oval
Heineken Ireland ■Sin É

Kinsale/Harbour Bar■

CELTIC SEA

■ Breweries/ Cidermakers
■ Pubs

ÁRAINN MHÓR BREWING COMPANY

Árainn Mhór Island, Burton Port, County Donegal
T: +353 (0)87 630 6856
W: www.ambrewco.com
E: info@ambrewco.com

The man behind Árainn Mhór Brewing Company is Gerry Forrest, whose work had involved supporting small-business start-ups.

After helping many such ventures, he felt he would like to start his own and began to think about what line to go into. He had come across craft beers from breweries on the Isles of Arran and Islay in Scotland and thought something similar might work in Ireland. As Gerry had been visiting the island of Árainn Mhór, off County Donegal's west coast, for years, the idea of a craft brewery, there just gelled.

Gerry secured a feasibility grant from Údarás na Gaeltachta, an

organisation that seeks to create economic development in the Gaeltacht (the Irish-speaking heartlands) to enable people to live and work in those areas. Before committing capital to a brewery, there was a need to establish whether the project was feasible – could the products sell? He visited many breweries and eventually secured the services of a Belgian brewer who is known as one of the foremost microbrewers in Europe. The brewer is brewing the first few batches of beers based on recipes developed in conjunction with Gerry. With the high regard worldwide for Belgian beer it seems a good place to start.

The initial stages have gone well and Gerry has been overwhelmed by the very positive response to the beers. Short-term plans are to set up a visitors' centre on the island and then, over time as income is consolidated, to install and establish a brewery on the island. In the longer-term, the plans are to have a full-scale craft brewery based on the island. This would create some local employment and bring more visitors to this beautiful island off the west coast of Donegal.

Availability
Currently there are two beers in production, both bottle-conditioned ales and they are available in counties Donegal and Sligo as well as in selected outlets in Dublin. There are hopes to increase availability throughout the northern half of the island of Ireland in 2007.

Visiting
No brewing currently takes place on Árainn Mhór but there are plans to have a visitors' centre there by summer 2007.

BÁN
Golden ale
Alcohol: 4.2%

RUA
Irish red ale
Alcohol: 4.2%

Bán (Irish for 'light' or 'white') is a golden ale, more in the European than British style and was chosen to compete in the lager market. The label features a golden sunset over the island.

The grist is made up of pilsner and Munich malts together with caramalt. East Kent Goldings hops are added at the start of the boil and at ten minutes in.

Bán pours a straw yellow colour and has a fresh, breezy nose bursting with tropical fruit and a hint of new mown hay. The palate is also fresh and fruity with a delicate but developing bitterness in the quenching finish. Bán is a lovely beer, perfect refreshment for the golden days of summer. It is an excellent apéritif or a match for soft cheeses.

Irish for 'red', Rua is a darker brew, complementing the lighter coloured Bán, with the label depicting a red sunset over the island. Pilsner malt and roasted barley make up the grist while glucose sugar is also added. East Kent Goldings are the kettle hops with Saaz at boil end.

Rua is a deep copper-coloured beer with an apple and pear fruitiness on the nose. There is a nuttiness on the palate as well as a grapefruit tang which carries through to a quite bitter finish. Although described as an Irish red ale, Rua is probably too bitter and lacking in sweetness to be a true representative of the style and is in fact closer to a pale ale or bitter.

BEAMISH & CRAWFORD

BEAMISH AND CRAWFORD PLC

South Main Street, Cork T: +353 (0)21 4911100 W: www.beamish.ie E: consumercare@beamish.ie

The bustling Beamish and Crawford brewery has occupied its present site on the banks of the River Lee for over two hundred years. The area was the heart of medieval Cork and a stone on which severed heads from the old jail that stood nearby were displayed can still be seen outside the counting house today. The counting house stands at the front of the brewery and is a beautiful Tudor-style building that was built in the 1920s that is just as impressive on the inside. The rest of the buildings are a mix of old and new, the legacy of various modernisation plans and changes in ownership and priorities. For the majority of its existence, the brewery enjoyed huge success but fortunes during the second half of the twentieth century were rather more mixed. However, with sales of the famous Beamish stout increasing, the future is looking bright for this famous brewery.

Brewing is first recorded on the site in 1645 but may well predate this. By 1715, Aylmer Allen had acquired the site and set up Allen's Brewery. It was from his son, Edward Allen, that the partnership of Messrs Beamish, Crawford, Barrett, and O'Brien would initially rent the brewery, laying the foundation for one of the world's famous stouts.

William Beamish and William Crawford were two northern Protestants who had come south to set up a butter and beef business in Cork. However, the influx of English porter changed their priorities and they joined in partnership with Richard Barrett and Digby O'Brien – who were already ale brewers – to become porter brewers. The partnership agreement is dated 13 January 1792 and the company was known as The Cork Porter Brewery.

O'Brien died shortly afterwards and Barrett retired in 1798, leaving the company in the hands of the Beamish and Crawford families.

Heavy initial investment included the employment of a number of men with backgrounds in London porter brewing. The business quickly went from strength to strength to become the largest brewery in Ireland, growing from an initial output of 12,000 barrels a year to 100,000 by 1805. The brewery was completely rebuilt and modernised in 1865 and it became a limited company in 1895 with all shares owned by the two families.

Growth continued into the early twentieth century with a number of acquisitions. 1901 saw the acquisition of Lane's Brewery, which stood over the road from Beamish and Crawford. In 1906 it was the turn of the St Stephen's Brewery at Dungarvan to be taken over and in 1914 Allman, Dowden and Company from Bandon was purchased, becoming bottlers for Beamish and Crawford.

A six-week strike in 1920 closed the brewery, the only time it has ever stopped brewing. This had a long-term impact on the company's fortunes as it gave Guinness an opportunity to gain a foothold in Cork. Previously the tied house

system (where a pub was tied to a brewery and therefore its products) operated in Cork and worked to keep Guinness at bay. However, with no beer available due to the strike the company had to let its publicans buy their beer from elsewhere. As the strike also affected the other big Cork brewery, Murphy's, there was only one company left for publicans to turn to. Guinness stepped in to supply the beer, finally getting the chance it had been looking for to get into the Cork market.

Beamish and Crawford was also an ale brewery for some time supplying British troops. However, following the troops' withdrawal from Ireland, ale brewing was phased out, finally ending in the 1930s.

The first half of the twentieth century were fairly good times for the company, who also acquired the Jenners Brewery in south London during this time, and efforts were made during this time to export Beamish Stout all over the world.

However, it was not to last. The 1950s were lean times for the company, which by this time were only brewing one product: stout. Guinness, spying a chance to swallow up another competitor, made a bid for the company as did a London financier, but it was Canadian Breweries of Toronto that was successful and took control in 1962. A massive investment programme followed, when many of the old brewery buildings were demolished

and state-of-the-art equipment was installed. Under Canadian Breweries' ownership, the brewery began brewing Carling Black Label lager in 1964 and a keg ale called 'Celebration'. In 1967, the British brewing giant Bass Charrington entered into an agreement with Canadian Breweries and managed the plant though a subsidiary called United Breweries. Shortly after this, in 1968, the waning popularity of Celebration ale led it to be replaced by Bass ale, which rapidly grew to occupy nearly a fifth of the draught ale market. In 1973, the brewing of Carlsberg lager under licence was added to the portfolio of beers being brewed.

By the late 1970s, Murphy's, the other Cork brewery, was in severe financial difficulties. Negotiations began between Beamish and Crawford and Murphy's to merge the two operations, though Beamish and Crawford were reluctant due to the financial state of their competitor. The deal, had it been successful, would have led to Beamish and Crawford taking over management of their competitor and possibly overall control. The deal was rejected by Murphy's shareholders and the two breweries still remain in separate hands.

In 1987, Canadian Breweries themselves were purchased by Elders IXL, the forerunners of the Foster's Brewing Group, resulting in Foster's lager being brewed on site though the brewing of Carlsberg ceased. By 1995, ownership had changed again and Beamish and Crawford became part of Scottish Courage, the brewing division of Scottish & Newcastle plc and a year later another lager began to be brewed under licence on the site – Miller Genuine Draft.

Lean times appear to be a thing of the past as not only are sales of stout increasing but also the brewery is set for further investment. A first-class kegging facility is being installed, further proof that the brewery is facing the twenty-first century in rude health.

Availability

Beamish Stout is widely available throughout Ireland, especially in Munster, while France, Finland and Portugal are the key markets in Europe. It can also be found in the UK, much of the rest of continental Europe, the US, South Africa, Australia and New Zealand with Eastern Europe and Russia emerging as new markets. Beamish Stout is mainly a draught product but cans are also available which replicate the draught's creamy head. Some limited bottling is done but it is hard to find and available only in Ireland. Beamish Irish Red is a draught-only product and rather more limited in its availability, being mainly found around Cork in Ireland with the UK and France being the international markets.

Visiting

Individuals and groups can visit the Beamish and Crawford brewery.

Groups can pre-book a time or join one of the organised visits which take place at 10.30 am and noon every Tuesday and Thursday, May to September, and 11 on Thursdays only from October to April. Visitors are entertained in the Beamish Hospitality Suite, where they see an audio-visual presentation and learn about the brewing process. The visit ends with a complimentary drink.

Brewing at Beamish & Crawford

The brewery is a mix of old and new, with a maze of pipework connecting the various parts of the four acre site. The original brewhouse is still there behind the counting house but is now largely an empty shell save for one old mash tun. The brewhouse was stripped bare by Canadian Breweries and a new facility was built with

more up-to-date equipment. Some of the fermentation vessels installed by Canadian Breweries now lie redundant themselves with closed conical fermenters having taken their place.

The brewery operates twenty-four hours a day, five days a week and is able to produce around 370 hectolitres in each brew. There are six or seven brews per day, adding up to a yearly output of over half a million hectolitres.

The pale malt is sourced locally from the Malting Company of Ireland in Cork. The mains water, which has historically been used for the brewing liquor, is demineralised before salts are added according to product specifications. A well exists on the site and was used for ale brewing in the 1800s and early 1900s before this product was phased out. A desalination plant has recently been installed, and this may lead to the well being used again as a source of brewing liquor.

The mashing regime varies by beer but both stout and red ale have an upward step infusion mash. For the stout the mash has a number of steps and lasts around ninety minutes. It starts at 45°C and is held at that temperature for thirty minutes. It is then increased stepwise over time, held at certain temperatures and finished at 76°C. The red ale follows a simpler mashing regime, it starts at around 65°C for thirty minutes before being increased to 77°C for the final

stages. The wort is then clarified in a lauter tun on the way to the wort receiver. The spent grains from the lauter tun go to a local farmer for animal feed.

In the brew kettle, the wort is pressure-boiled at 104°C for seventy minutes and hopped with pellets. The hopped wort is then clarified via a whirlpool before being cooled to 14°C. A brewing syrup derived from maize is also added in the brew kettle to enhance the final flavour and provide extra fermentable material, as the brewery operates a system of 'elevated strength brewing' for reasons of energy efficiency and capacity.

Elevated strength brewing means that the hopped wort is fermented to around twice the alcoholic strength of the finished beer. The beer is fermented in closed conicals with both the stout and red ale using the original Beamish and Crawford yeast strain. Fermentation lasts three days and then the red ale is centrifuged to remove any remaining solid particles before being chilled to –1°C, filtered and conditioned. The stout is not filtered as isinglass finings are added to the fermentation vessel. The stout is drawn off the bottom of the cone and circulated back in further up generating a current that blends in the finings. The brew then rests for twelve hours, allowing the finings to gather the yeast to the bottom of the cone where it is drawn off and sent to the yeast recovery plant. The stout is also centrifuged before conditioning.

Both products emerge from fermentation with some conditioning and therefore may only need to spend twenty-four hours in the conditioning tank. This is a minimum and often more time is given. Both beers are conditioned at –1°C so that any remaining sediment will fall to the bottom and any chill haze can be removed. The beers are then pumped to the bright beer tank where the strong beer is reduced in alcoholic strength. This is done by blending the beer with highly purified, de-mineralised and de-aerated brewing liquor by means of a centrifuge. The finished beer is then held in the bright beer tank for twenty-four hours at –1°C. All products are pasteurised and kegging and bottling are done on site but canning is carried out elsewhere. A tasting panel convenes at around midday each day to test each batch before and after packaging and it must pass this final test before being released from the brewery.

Beamish and Crawford also brew Fosters lager and two other lagers under licence – Carling and Miller Genuine Draft.

are the canned products. The hard-to-find bottle is carbonated, giving a slightly different experience and one worth looking out for.

BEAMISH STOUT

Irish dry stout
Alcohol: 4.3%

Beamish stout is one of the great historic Irish stouts. It is brewed predominantly with pale malt with 10 percent malted wheat for head retention, 10 percent roasted barley for the classic roasted stout taste and a dash of black malt for colour. Target and Northern Brewer hops are used for bittering and ten minutes from boil-end, there is an addition of English Goldings.

Beamish Stout is black with burgundy highlights and a creamy-coloured head. There is a good roasted, almost smoky, character on the nose with some coffee and chocolate notes. The palate is decidedly roasty with hints of chocolate and cream, and there is a good level of bitterness in the lengthy finish that is also reminiscent of black coffee. This is a very lovely and enjoyable stout.

On draught, it is nitrogenated, as

BEAMISH RED

Irish red ale
Alcohol: 4.2%

Beamish Red is a relatively recent development that was first brewed around the mid-1990s. It is brewed from a grist of pale malt, crystal malt for sweetness and a small amount of black malt for colouring. Target hops are added at the start of the boil; there are no late hops. The flavour predominantly comes from the malt and a small quantity of lactose sugar added during the boil that contributes sweetness and smoothness of body.

This nitrogenated beer pours a reddish-amber colour with an off-white head. A malty, lightly-fruity nose with overtones of toffee leads to a lightly-bodied and malty palate. The finish is light with restrained bitterness making for a very soft interpretation of an Irish red ale.

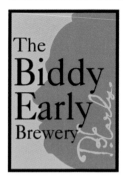

BIDDY EARLY BREWERY

Inagh, Ennis, County Clare
T: +353 (0)65 683 6742
W: www.beb.ie
E: info@beb.ie

The Biddy Early brewpub stands on a crossroads in the remote hamlet of Inagh in County Clare. There has been a pub here for over two hundred years, operating as a shebeen for a good part of that time. In the past, many travellers and farmers going to market would have quenched their thirst at the pub. Nowadays it is on the tourist route to the nearby majestic Cliffs of Moher and the magical Burren in north Clare. However, for those wanting to experience excellent craft beer, Biddy is an attraction in itself.

Biddy Early is named after a local wise woman, but it took a wise man to turn it into a brewpub. That man was Dr Peadar Garvey, a retired industrial chemist. The pub had been in the Garvey family since 1983 and when Dr Garvey retired in 1994, he ran the pub full time. He soon became a bit bored with just running a pub and, inspired by a brewpub he saw in the Isle of Man, thought he would give brewing a go. As a result, the Biddy Early Brewpub opened in 1995 and was the forerunner of the first wave of craft breweries in Ireland. His son, Niall Garvey, took over in 1997 after his father's untimely death.

Being an accountant by trade

Niall Garvey and his brews

makes him an unlikely candidate to be a craft brewer. However, Niall learnt his brewing on the job with some formal training in England. In 1998, he oversaw a large expansion when outbuildings were acquired to house part of the brewing process, thus increasing capacity. The expansion allowed Biddy to bottle its beer and sell it beyond the brewpub.

Initially the beers enjoyed great success due to their novelty and attempts were made to find outlets far and wide. However, more recently, the Garveys decided to restrict the sale of their beers to those who really want to sell it and also to concentrate on export.

Availability
Draught Biddy is only available at the brewpub whilst bottled Biddy can be found in Fawls pub in Ennis and O'Briens Kitchen in Lahinch, both in County Clare, McCambridges in Galway and some excellent independent wine merchants in Dublin. Overseas, Biddy is available in Tokyo, in the US via Michael Jackson's Rare Beer Club and in Ottawa, Canada. Cask-conditioned versions also make their way to the UK from time to time, particularly for beer festivals.

Visiting
Being a pub, it is open all year round but brewery tours are available for those wanting to know more about the brewing process. The tours are available throughout the year round for groups, whilst individuals are catered for from the middle of May to the middle of September each year. Both individuals and groups must make a prior booking. The visit will include an audiovisual presentation and a tour of the brewery, followed by a sample of the beers.

Brewing Biddy's Beer
Before 1998, all the brewing was done in a tiny space in a corner of the pub. Purchasing the outbuildings increased Biddy's capacity tenfold. Brewing still takes place in the pub, in a room known as the brew kitchen, whilst fermentation and conditioning happens in the outbuildings.

The brew kitchen is very compact and it is hard to believe the whole brewing process once took place here. The original mash tun and brew kettle remain but expansion brought new fermenters and conditioning tanks. These fermenters are twice the size of the brew kitchen's seven hectolitre

capacity and therefore they have to double-brew to fill them. In a year, Biddy brews around five thousand hectolitres, which is distributed fairly evenly between its brews, with Red Biddy slightly ahead of the pack. In winter, brewing takes place around twice a week, though this can rise to a full seven days in the summer. Biddy prides itself on using natural and, where possible, Irish ingredients.

Indeed it tries to source as locally as possible to give the beer a local flavour in more ways than one. 95% of the grain used is Irish, from either the Malting Company of Ireland or Minch Norton, but the lack of speciality malts in Ireland means the brewery has no choice but to get these from England. Biddy can call on its own spring water for brewing liquor, which comes out at about halfway between a good ale and good lager water. Therefore some salts are added for lager brewing whilst it is burtonised for the other beers.

Mashing lasts ninety minutes. Blonde Biddy lager is mashed at 62°C whilst the other beers are mashed at 69°C. The wort is then transferred to the direct-fired brew kettle, in which the lager is boiled for seventy minutes, with the other beers getting the full ninety minutes. The hops are a mixture of whole cone and pellet and Carrageen Moss – a seaweed picked on a beach ten miles away at Liscannor Bay – is used to fine, or clarify, the hopped wort in the kettle. The solids cling to the seaweed as the hopped wort goes through the whirlpool.

The hopped wort is then pumped to the outbuildings via a heat exchanger. Hopped wort destined to be lager is cooled to 8°C, for the other beers a temperature around 20°C is required. As the hopped wort passes through the heat exchanger, it warms up the cold water, which is then sent to the hot liquor tank, ready for the next mash.

The lager will be fermented in closed conical tank for ten days with the temperature rising to 16°C. The other beers are open fermented for four days and held at 20°C. Two main yeasts are used, one for lager and one for the other beers: both are the original strains from 1995 and are stored at Galway University. For seasonal brews and one-offs, dried yeast is bought as required.

The green beer is then cooled to as close to 0°C as possible for conditioning. The lager is conditioned for four weeks and the others as long as possible, a minimum of one week but preferably two. The beer is then sent to the bright beer tank after most of the yeast has fallen out of suspension. The lager is, however, filtered en route. In the bright beer tank the carbonation is adjusted and the beer is then kegged. All the bottled products are sterile filtered.

As well as three regular beers, Biddy brews a number of seasonal beers and one-offs which are only available in the brewpub. These include: Pale Biddy, an excellent assertively-hoppy pale ale; White Biddy, a tart wheat beer in the Belgian style; and Buzzy Biddy, a honey beer using the nectar of bees from the nearby Aillwee Caves in the Burren. In 2005 Biddy celebrated ten years of brewing, and to commemorate this a limited quantity of each year's best seasonal beer is bottled for a wider audience. These are bottle-conditioned and labelled 'Biddy Birthday Beer' or 'Triple B'.

BLONDE BIDDY

Pilsner-style lager
Alcohol: 4.2%

Blonde Biddy is brewed entirely with Irish lager malt. It is hopped with Nugget and Target for bittering with the classic noble lager hops of Hersbrucker and Saaz added for aroma at the boil end.

With a light golden colour and a floral, noble hop aroma, Blonde Biddy has a classic lager nose joined by some toasted malt. Spicy and tangy in the mouth, it delivers a clean and quenching finish with a delicate but firm lingering bitterness. Blonde Biddy is an excellent interpretation of the pilsner style and a good companion for lightly battered fish, or indeed can also be used as an ingredient in the batter itself.

RED BIDDY

Irish red ale
Alcohol: 4.9%

This is an Irish red ale with a difference. Its use of local herbs and plants harks back to the traditional way of flavouring ale before the use of hops became widespread in Ireland.

Pale malt makes up the majority of the grist with a good quantity of crystal malt and a dash of chocolate malt for colouring. There is only one hop addition – Challenger hops are added at the start of the boil for bittering. Just before the end of the boil, the herb bog myrtle is added for flavour. This was a traditional ingredient in beer before the introduction of hops and is handpicked from Mount Callan, the mountain at the back of the brewery –

you cannot get any more local or fresher than that.

Red Biddy has a cream coloured head atop a reddish-brown body. The nose is highly complex – malty, dark fruits, burnt caramel, a sage-like herbal quality and no doubt more besides. There is some malty sweetness on the palate with more burnt caramel and some toasted malt. The finish is malty, roasty and herbal with a delicate bitterness. Red Biddy is without doubt one of the best and most complex Irish red ales and is truly one of Ireland's great beers. Its herbal quality makes it a good ingredient in stews. It can also be a match for strong cheeses and even chocolate, while its robust flavours would stand up well to roasted red meats.

The bottled version is carbonated whilst on draught it is nitrogenated.

Nevertheless pale malt makes up the majority of the grist and is joined by flaked barley and chocolate malt. Pride, Galena and Nugget are the bittering hops with Fuggles added at boil end.

It pours black with reddish highlights and an orange-brown head. The complex nose is dominated by an assertive roastiness and a whiff of smoke. There are also dark chocolate and creamy notes with a hint of raisins. It is very roasty and creamy in the mouth with some dark chocolate bitterness that is also evident on the lasting, slightly malty, finish. A good level of bitterness makes this a classic example of an Irish dry stout and a good companion to shellfish.

The bottled version is carbonated whilst the draught is nitrogenated, making the draught version slightly sweeter and creamier.

BLACK BIDDY

Irish dry stout
Alcohol: 4.2%

This was the first beer brewed by Biddy and the first new stout brewed in Ireland for around two hundred years.

A good quantity of roasted barley, possibly more than most brewers would use, is the hallmark of Black Biddy.

CARLOW BREWING COMPANY

Seamus O'Hara behind the taps

CARLOW BREWING COMPANY

**The Old Goods Store,
Station Road, Carlow
T: +353 (0)59 913 4356
W: www.carlowbrewing.com
E: info@carlowbrewing.com**

Carlow lies in the barley growing region of the Barrow valley in the south east of Ireland – not a bad place to locate a brewery. The brewery was set up by brothers Seamus and Eamon O'Hara and brewing began in 1998 – the first time beer had been brewed in Carlow in over a hundred years. Seamus had been introduced to cask-conditioned real ale whilst working over in England. The brothers had also travelled in the US, where they had seen at first-hand the craft beer revolution there and thought that they would like to try setting up a craft brewery back home.

The brewery is located in the lovely old railway goods store that has stood next to Carlow railway station since 1846, when the railway reached the town. Originally, this would have been a busy place where goods were loaded and unloaded and it is good to see that the building has found a new use.

Early progress was slow as the brothers found it difficult to get their beers to the market in Ireland due to the dominance of the big brewers, a familiar tale. Initially the Irish drinking culture was also problematic: people were so used to seeing and drinking the same few mass-produced brands everywhere that it was difficult to gain a foothold. They therefore focussed on exports and found a great deal of interest in quality Irish craft beer overseas.

Winning gold and silver medals at the Brewing Industry International Awards in 2000 gave their beers great kudos and was a big step forward. Thankfully the Irish drinking culture is becoming more discerning, meaning that there is now rising demand for Carlow's beers in Ireland. The brewing capacity at Carlow is being increased and there are plans to expand and improve their distribution network on the island to meet the new demand for their beers.

Availability

Carlow beers are available on draught and in bottle. In Ireland, their products are mainly to be found in the on-trade in the Dublin and Carlow/Kilkenny areas, but are also available elsewhere, such as in Dundalk and Galway. In the off-trade they are listed by the Superquinn and Tesco supermarkets and can also be found in Oddbins and other good independent off-licences. Internationally, Carlow beers can be found in the UK – sometimes in cask-conditioned form – the US, Sweden, Finland, Denmark, Italy, France and Russia. They also brew an own label stout for Marks and Spencer, based on a different recipe to their regular stout.

Visiting

Groups are welcome to visit the brewery by appointment where they can see the brewing process and sample the beers in a purpose built bar. Anyone wishing to visit should contact the brewery to arrange their visit.

Brewing at Carlow

Another of the O'Hara clan, Michael, along with Liam Hanlon, are the current brewers. They run a brewery that can produce 15 hectolitres per batch and currently brew around 4,500 hectolitres a year. Brewing usually takes place three to four days a week – often brewing twice a day – and this is set to increase further. The stout and wheat beer each make up around 40 percent of the total output with the red ale taking up the remaining 20 percent.

Currently, due to capacity constraints at Carlow, some of their beer is brewed under contract by Beamish and Crawford in Cork. This quantity is, however, in decline, and they expect that increasing capacity at Carlow will bring the arrangement to an end very soon.

The pale malt is sourced locally from Minch Norton a few miles up the road in Athy and the brewing liquor is drawn from the municipal supply. Being fairly hard, it is carbon-filtered and then burtonised to the correct specification.

The grist and liquor is mashed in at 60°C and this rises to 76°C during the ninety minute mash. The hops added during the boil are in pellet form with Challenger being the bittering hop added at the start of the boil. The boil lasts between an hour and seventy-five minutes during which there are two further hop additions. The hopped wort is clarified in a whirlpool, which separates out the hop residues and trub, before the hopped wort passes through a heat exchanger to be cooled to around 20°C, ready for fermentation.

The brewery has three closed conical fermenters and uses the same yeast for each of its beers. The yeast contributes fruity flavours and aromas but is not an overly dominant characteristic of the final beer. Fermentation typically lasts three to four days and is held at 20°C as the yeast strain is somewhat vigorous.

Once fermentation is complete, the green beer is crash cooled down to just above 0°C and kept in this condition for two days, at which point much of the yeast drops out of suspension. The beer is then transferred to the conditioning tanks that are kept in the cold store and will condition for two weeks.

The draught beer is then filtered and kegged. Unfortunately, space does not allow for a bottling line so beer destined for bottles is tankered in an unfiltered state to England where it will be filtered and pasteurised before bottling.

suggesting that the Celts used a proportion of wheat in brewing their beer.

When Curim was introduced, no other Irish brewer was making a wheat beer, so this was something to differentiate Carlow from other brewers. Curim is not currently available in the US.

The grist is made of pale malt, caramalt, wheat malt and torrefied wheat. Curim is only lightly hopped with an addition of Mount Hood at the mid-point and Cascade at the end. It pours a good golden colour with a muted but fruity nose, with apples and pears dominant. The palate is clean with a hint of fruit and spice and the finish delivers some tartness and a delicate hop bitterness. Curim is rather more hoppy than most wheat beers and makes for a refreshing beer that could pair well with moderately spicy foods.

CURIM

South German-style filtered wheat beer
Alcohol: 4.3%

The name is derived from the old Celtic word for beer and is inspired by archaeological evidence

MOLINGS

Irish red ale
Alcohol: 4.3%

Molings is known as O'Hara's Red in the US but the name Moling comes from the famous Book of Moling that sits alongside the Book of Kells in Trinity College Dublin. It is a beautifully crafted illuminated manuscript and dates from the eighth century CE, written by the monks of St Molings Monastery in County Carlow.

Pale malt is joined by crystal malt, caramalt and roasted barley for character, sweetness and colour. The mid-point hop addition is Willamette with Mount Hood then added at boil end. Molings is a deep reddish colour, exhibiting a whiff of toastiness from the roasted barley and a light berry fruitiness with raspberries to the fore on the nose. It has a great robustly flavoured malty palate, featuring dark fruits and a roasted flavour. The finish is roasty again with a good hop bitterness. Molings is different to most interpretations of Irish red ale, being more hoppy and having less malty sweetness. Its robust nature would make it a good companion for roasted red meats and stews.

O'HARA'S CELTIC STOUT

Irish dry stout
Alcohol: 4.3%

Initially Carlow were reluctant to brew a stout due to the dominance of the big brewers' versions. However, they decided to brew a more full-flavoured 'old fashioned' style of stout and were rewarded when O'Hara's won both a gold medal in the stout and mild category and the overall Champion Trophy at the Brewing Industry International Awards in 2000 – a great feat for a small brewery.

It is brewed with pale malt, caramalt, roasted barley and flaked barley with a mid-point hop addition of Fuggles, followed by Styrian Goldings at the end of the boil.

The bottled version is jet black with a beige head. The nose is tremendously complex with smokiness and roastiness dominant, but there are also creamy notes. In the mouth, O'Hara's is very roasty with an almost charcoal-like flavour, bitter with some creamy malt. The finish is lingering and has all that would be expected of an Irish dry stout – a good roasted bitterness that dries the mouth. O'Hara's is a great stout, its assertive bitterness and fullness of flavour would make it stand up well to game dishes. The draught version is nitrogenated.

CELTIC BREW

**Clonard, Enfield,
County Meath
T: +353 (0)44 937 5312
E: sales@premierbeers.ie**

Celtic Brew is the brainchild of Dean McGuinness. His family has been in the drinks trade for thirty-five years, starting out in the UK off-trade as wholesalers. In the late '80s, they took over Continental Lager Distributors – a firm importing European beers. When they took on Samuel Adams, the excellent American craft lager, Dean came into contact with the craft brewing scene in the US and was inspired to start brewing back in Ireland.

Celtic Brew is based in an industrial unit on the edge of the village of Enfield in County Meath. Launched in April 1997, it was one of the early members of the first wave of Irish craft brewing. The initial plan was modest – a ten hectolitre system to brew draught beers for around twenty pubs. However, such is Guinness' control over the on-trade, Dean was forced to look at bottling. This actually proved to be a positive step and it was quickly apparent that

the ten hectolitre system would not be large enough and was replaced before it was even used.

In common with the other first wave craft brewers, Celtic brewed a lager, stout and red ale under the 'Finians' range, with the company's logo of an Irish wolfhound featuring prominently on the label. In addition to this, two lagers that were not part of the Finians range were also brewed and were supplemented by various contract brews. Dean does not contract brew simply to generate revenue, but as part of a deeper philosophy. For Dean, contract brewing creates a multiplicity of beers that can raise awareness of craft brewing in Ireland, which means that people do not have to stick to the same old brands. To date, Dean believes he has brewed a total of thirty-six beers.

Though contract brewing continues, the Finians range of beers have been brewed for the last time. The future for Celtic Brew is to create new and interesting niche beers to be ahead of people's tastes, rather than accept the market as it is by brewing the usual three – lager, red ale and stout. Work on the exciting redevelopment of Celtic Brew's beers is ongoing at the time of writing.

Availability

Brewing is temporarily on hold though some of Celtic Brew's beers can still be found in the independent off-trade throughout the Republic of Ireland. The Finians range was available in the UK, France, Germany, Sweden, Italy, Spain, Australia and Japan and it is anticipated that the new beers will also be available in these countries when they are launched.

Visiting
The brewery is not open to the public.

Brewing

Dean McGuinness trained at the Institute of Brewing in Chicago. He is assisted from time to time by Steve Griffin, a brewing consultant who works for big companies such as Anheuser Busch, SAB/Miller and Chang, as well as craft brewers.

The original ten-hectolitre system was replaced by the current twenty-five-hectolitre one, and yearly production is around five thousand hectolitres. The brewhouse is split between two floors with the mash tun and brewkettle on one floor and the conical fermentation vessels, conditioning tanks and bright beer tank housed underneath on a lower floor.

Currently there is only contract brewing taking place, usually about twice a week, but a double brew is done on each of these days. The local mains water is hard, so it is softened for brewing liquor before being burtonised as required.

Many of the contract brews are lagers and tend to be mashed for an hour at around 65°C. The false bottom of the mash tun is removed and the wort is strained through a perforated plate. Pellet hops are added in the brew kettle and the lagers receive a seventy-five minute boil. A whirlpool separates the hopped wort from the hop residue and trub and it is then cooled to 11°C.

Fermentation lasts around a week and is not allowed to rise above 16°C. The green beer is then cooled to 6°C and the yeast removed. It is then further cooled to around 0°C and conditions in the same tank for one and a half to two weeks. After the rougher alcohols have evaporated, the tank is capped to build up as much natural carbonation as possible. Carbonation will then be adjusted before the beer is filtered on its way to the bright beer tank. The beer is usually flash-pasteurised and bottled.

COLLEGE GREEN BREWERY

**1 College Green Mews,
Belfast BT7 1LN
Contact the Hilden Brewery
for any enquiries regarding
College Green Brewery**

Just behind Queen's University, on
the buzzing Botanic Avenue, is the
College Green Brewery and Molly's
Yard restaurant. They occupy the
outbuildings of the recently renovated
College Green House.

College Green House dates from
1870 and lists amongst its early
occupants John McConnell,
managing director of Dunville's
Distillery in Belfast. The house was
divided into flats in the 1930s,
becoming the residence of artistic
types. By the late 1990s the City
Council declared the house
uninhabitable and it was closed.
Hearth, a charity that specialises in
restoring old buildings of
architectural merit for dwellings,
acquired a long lease in 2000 and set
about restoring the building with aid
from the Heritage Lottery Fund.

The Scullion family from Hilden
Brewery became interested in the
then dilapidated outbuildings and
with some foresight saw their
potential. As 2005 came to a close,
Molly's Yard restaurant opened in the
former stables. The brewery will be
housed in the compact old coach
house and the brewing vessels,
acquired from a Belfast brewpub that
was never to be, are in place. Brewing

should hopefully get under way in 2007, but the draught products are already available as they are currently brewed at Hilden. There are also plans to bottle the beers, with the exception of Belfast Blonde.

Availability
The draught ales can currently be found in Molly's Yard restaurant, occasionally at the John Hewitt bar in Belfast and the Dirty Duck pub in Holywood, County Down.

Visiting
The brewery is not yet up and running but its size will probably preclude any visits. However, behind the wooden front doors are a set of glass doors which reveal the workings of the brewery. When it is up and running, the plan is to swing the wooden doors open to reveal the brewery.

BELFAST BLONDE
Lager-style beer
Alcohol: 4.3%

Belfast Blonde was created to cater for restaurant customers wishing to drink lager. However, it is actually a hybrid beer. It is fermented with an ale yeast so is technically an ale but brewed as a lager. Lager malt and a small quantity of crystal make up the grist with some maize to counteract the malt, leading to a cleaner finished beer. Classic lager hops Saaz and Hersbrucker are added at the start and again towards the end of the boil. The beer is conditioned in cellar tanks before being filtered and kegged. There are plans to switch to a lager yeast soon making this a fully-fledged lager.

The current brew is carbonated and dispensed through a lager-style font. It is pale gold in colour and has a fruity nose, with dessert apples prominent and some spicy hints underneath. The palate is mildly spicy and a light hop bitterness characterises the dry, spicy and refreshing finish. Belfast Blonde is an enjoyable, quenching beer that would be a good apéritif to a meal at Molly's Yard.

HEADLESS DOG
English-style bitter
Alcohol: 4.3%

At the foot of the wall between the brewhouse and the door to the restaurant is a longstanding painted mural of a headless dog. The mural is actually the logo of the Vacuum, an alternative Belfast monthly newspaper. Why it was painted on that wall is a bit of a mystery but it is the inspiration behind the naming of this brew. Pale, crystal and Munich malt make up the grist, Cascade and Northdown hops are added at the start of the boil with Progress at the end.

Headless Dog is a cask-conditioned amber-gold beer with nutty, earthy and fruity (apple and pear) characteristics on the nose. The nuttiness is also found on the palate with a hoppy tang. The finish is mouth-drying with a good and developing bitterness, making Headless Dog a fine example of the style.

First Gold are all added at the start of the boil but, to get that extra chocolate flavour, some cocoa powder is also added to the brew kettle.

This cask-conditioned beer is dark tawny in colour and not totally opaque. The bouquet is wonderfully enticing with cocoa, dark chocolate and roasted grain intermingling beautifully. More dark chocolate is found on the palate as is a hint of tart fruit. The finish has a pronounced cocoa flavour and a bitter dark chocolate dryness. Molly's Chocolate Stout would work well either as an after dinner drink or to accompany chocolate-based desserts. This is an excellent beer – seek out and enjoy.

MOLLY'S CHOCOLATE STOUT

Alcohol: 4.2%

This chocolate stout derives from a desire to do something different to the usual stout. The malts are pale and chocolate with some malted whole oats added as well. There is no late hopping – Challenger, Goldings and

FRANCISCAN WELL BREWERY

14 North Mall, Cork City
T: +353 (0)21 421 0130
W: www.franciscanwellbrewery.com
E: info@franciscanwellbrewery.com

The Franciscan Well craft brewery and brewpub is announced by a sign above an archway on Cork's North Mall depicting a rather pleased-looking monk with a tankard of ale. The monk and the brewery's name have their origin in the fact that this is the site of a former Franciscan monastery. There is also a Holy Well on the back wall of what is now the beer garden, dating back to 1219.

Over the years the site has been home to a mineral water company and even a printing press. For a long time there has been a pub on the site and, when the current owner Liam McNeill took over, things began to change.

Liam had seen for himself the success of craft brewing and brewpubs in the US and UK that offered quality locally crafted beers and increased choice for the drinker. This was also the time when the first wave of Irish craft brewing was rising with Biddy Early and the Porterhouse already established as brewpubs. Both these events inspired the opening of the brewery and brewpub in 1998.

Since then, the Franciscan Well has gone from strength to strength and now supplies a number of other bars with its draught beers. The range has broadened from three initial beers to five regular brews, joined by seasonal specialities. Occasionally one of the products is available in the bar as a cask-conditioned beer. There are plans to increase the frequency of this and get guest cask-conditioned beers from other breweries such as Messrs Maguires and Hilden.

Availability

Franciscan Well beers are available on draught in a number of Cork City pubs as well as in Dublin [at] The Ginger Man, Paddy Cullens, Mary Macs and Hobblers End. They can also be found in Maggie Mays, Wexford and O'Shea's in Sneem, County Kerry. Check the website for an up-to-date list of outlets. The beer is not bottled but five-litre mini kegs are available for the take-home market. Cask-conditioned beer can be bought wholesale via the Hilden Brewery.

Visiting

It is possible to visit the brewhouse on most days and learn about the brewing process. The visit will also include a tasting of the range. However, anyone interested must book in advance.

Brewing at the Franciscan Well

The head brewer is Russell Garet who came to Cork to help install the new brewery and ended up staying on. He previously worked in a number of craft breweries in the US and has brewing qualifications from the Institutes of Brewing in Chicago and London.

The brewhouse sits in the corner of the beer garden and its glass frontage means people can see the brewery and the goings-on inside.

However, a 6am start usually means that Russell has finished brewing by the time the pub opens. The brewhouse is capable of brewing over eleven hectolitres in one brew and the output for the year is about a thousand hectolitres in total, with around 60 percent of this being sold in the pub. Russell brews around once

or twice a week during the winter but this increases to three times in the summer months.

The mains water from a local reservoir provides the brewing liquor and is untreated, save for being filtered. The pale and lager malt both come from the Malting Company of

Ireland based in Cork. The mash is heated in the mash kettle which also doubles as the brew kettle. The mashing temperature is strictly controlled depending on the brew. The Rebel Red Ale and Shandon Stout receive a standard infusion mash at around 67°C. The others have an upward-step mash, meaning that the start temperature is increased during the mash. Friar Weiss starts at 42°C to get the correct flavour compounds whereas the Rebel Lager and Blarney Blonde start ten degrees higher to get a complete breakdown of the sugars so that none remain in the final beer. The mashing temperature for the lager, blonde and weiss is increased to 60°C and then to 67°C. Mashing lasts ninety minutes though Friar Weiss gets an extra thirty, due to the use of wheat malt.

Once mashing is complete the mash is sent to the mash tun, which has a perforated bottom for draining. The mash is recirculated over the mash bed of spent grains to extract more sugar and clarify the wort. A local farmer then collects the spent grains for cattle feed.

The mash kettle now becomes the brew kettle and the wort is boiled for seventy-five minutes, during which the pellet hops are added. The hopped wort then goes through a whirlpool to separate out the hops and any trub before cooling by heat exchanger.

All the fermenters are closed conicals but two are double the size of the mash/brew kettle. This means that when brewing the best sellers – Blarney Blonde and Rebel Red Ale – Russell has to double brew to fill the fermenters. Three yeast cultures are used and usually renewed twice a year. Friar Weiss is fermented using a Bavarian wheat beer yeast culture from the famous Weihenstephan Brewing Institute in Munich and a Danish lager yeast takes care of Rebel Lager. The ale yeast has an interesting heritage, originating in the old Ballantines Brewery in the US. After

Ballantines closed, the yeast was taken to the highly rated Sierra Nevada Brewery and the Franciscan Well were able to use this culture, which can impart a citrussy characteristic to the beer.

The fermenters are also the conditioning tanks and Rebel Lager will ferment for seven to ten days at around 12°C and the other beers for three to five days at 20-22°C. The beers are conditioned close to 0°C with the lager spending a total of twenty-one days in the brewery fermenting and conditioning. The other beers are ready to leave the brewery after two weeks.

The beer is drawn off from a tap halfway up the cone in the base of the tanks, leaving the yeast and other matter to settle below this point for easy removal. All the beer, with the exception of Friar Weiss, is then filtered but not microfiltered or pasteurised so as to retain flavour.

The beer rests in the bright beer tank where the natural carbonation from conditioning is adjusted upwards before being kegged. Blarney Blonde, Rebel Lager and Rebel Red Ale destined to be sold in the pub are not kegged but, interestingly, are housed in big tanks behind the bar, each containing around 13.5 hectolitres or 2,400 pints! It is the only pub in Ireland to store its beer in this way prior to serving.

As well as the five regulars there are also seasonal beers. Purgatory Pale Ale is usually available during the summer months and is a fully flavoured assertively hoppy, pale ale in the US style. Bellringer Winter Warmer is malty and warming for colder times of the year. Other seasonals are also planned.

The Franciscan Well brews what it calls 'naturally better beers': tradition and naturalness are watchwords as the preservatives, chemicals and processing aids often used by bigger brewers have no place here.

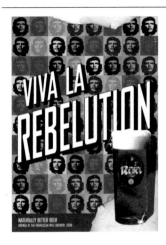

BLARNEY BLONDE

Kölsch-style beer
Alcohol: 4.2%

With a picture of Blarney Castle on the label, Blarney Blonde is different to other Irish beers as it is in the style of a German Kölsch beer. Kölsch, despite its looks, is an ale made by brewers in Cologne. Indeed, it is a protected name so that Kölsch can only be made in Cologne, anyone else making it must call it Kölsch-style beer. If only brewers in Plzen and Budweis had protected their names!.

Pale malt makes up 85 percent of the grist with the reminder being wheat malt. Perle hops are used for bittering with Hersbrucker added at boil end for aroma. Blarney Blonde has a full gold colour and has a soft sweet aroma of tropical fruits, a nose very reminiscent of new world chardonnay. The palate exhibits a delicate tropical fruitiness and the finish has a restrained hop bitterness. This is a lovely beer, refreshing and light, delicately fruity and a great interpretation of a Kölsch beer, which could be a fine match for delicate fish dishes.

REBEL LAGER

European-style Pilsner
Alcohol: 4.2%

Rebel Lager is made from lager malt only with no adjuncts. It is bittered by adding German Perle and the classic Saaz hops at the beginning of the boil, with more Saaz added at the end for that noble hop aroma expected in a good pilsner.

A light-gold coloured lager with a delicate floral aroma from the Saaz hop. There is also a hint of vanilla on the clean nose. There are crisp, spicy hops on the palate with some malty notes. The finish is slightly mouth-drying and has an excellent lasting bitterness. All in all a decent lager.

FRIAR WEISS

**South German style unfiltered wheat beer
Alcohol: 4.7%**

Wheat beer imported from Germany was selling so well in the pub that they thought they would have a go at brewing their own. A studious friar adorns the label of this beer which has 30 percent wheat malt. Pale malt makes up most of the remainder with a small quantity of crystal malt for colour. Cascade is the bittering hop with a small touch of Saaz and Hersbrucker added at the end of the boil.

Friar Weiss pours an orangey colour and has a deep yeasty cloudiness. There is a classic nose of intense banana, some lemon and a whiff of cloves. In the mouth there is tart fruit, ripe bananas and the desired yeast bite. Bananas again on the finish which is quenchingly tart and has a good crisp acidity. One of the best wheat beers made in Ireland featuring an exquisite balance between fruitiness and tartness, marvellous. This beer would accompany certain fruity, tangy desserts such as lemon meringue as well as a variety of dishes from seafood to chicken.

REBEL RED

Irish red ale
Alcohol: 4.3%

Rebel Red is made with 84 percent pale malt with a good dose of crystal and a touch of roasted barley. First Gold and Fuggles are the bittering hops with East Kent Goldings for aroma and flavour.

A reddish amber-brown ale with a lovely caramel and lightly fruity nose reminiscent of raisins or dark fruits. There are dark fruits in the mouth and the malty sweetness is balanced by a good hop bitterness. The finish is fruity and delicately bitter. A great Irish red ale of character, not too hoppy or bitter. Another excellent Franciscan Well brew that could go well with ribs or any dish with a sweetish sauce.

SHANDON STOUT

Irish dry stout
Alcohol: 4.3%

Named after the famous Shandon steeple on Cork's north side, this stout is made in the local Cork style. Seventy percent pale malt is joined by equal proportions of roasted barley and wheat malt, the latter to aid head retention. Target and First Gold hops

are added at the start of the boil with a second addition of First Gold halfway through the boil and ending with Fuggles at the boil end.

In common with other stouts, Shandon Stout is dispensed with a large quantity of nitrogen in the gas mix to get the expected creamy head. It pours black with red highlights and a dark beige head. The nose is lightly roasty and smoky with chocolate notes. There is a good roastiness on the palate joined by dark fruits and again possibly a hint of smokiness. The finish has a decent level of roasted bitterness, long-lasting with a hint of sour fruit, making for a good stout.

GUINNESS
St James's Gate Brewery

St James's Gate
Dublin 8
T: +353 (0)1 483 6700
W: www.guinness.com

The 31st of December, 1759 was a momentous day in the history of the brewing industry not only in Ireland but also in the world. It was the day Arthur Guinness took over a small brewery in Dublin, beginning a brewing dynasty, and leading to the creation of one of the most recognisable beers in the world.

Arthur Guinness was born in 1725 near Celbridge in County Kildare, son of Richard Guinness, Land Steward to the Archbishop of Cashel. One of Richard's duties was to supervise the brewing of small quantities of beer on the estate for the workers and the household, and Arthur may well have learnt brewing from his father.

Arthur's lucky break came when the Archbishop, Arthur's godfather, left him £100 in his will – a considerable sum at the time. With the money, Arthur ran a brewery in nearby Leixlip.

In 1759, he left the Leixlip brewery to his younger brother Richard and tried his luck in the capital city.

At the time Irish beer was subject to higher duty than that from Great Britain, leading the young Arthur to look at the possibility of brewing in Holyhead or Caernarfon in North Wales before settling on Dublin. He bought a small, dilapidated brewery covering a four-acre site from a Mark Rainsford, signing a 9,000-year lease at a rate of £45 a year. By 1769, he was exporting his ale to England: the first shipment contained six and a half barrels. The lease he signed granted him free access to water, but Dublin Corporation wanted to make him pay for it and in 1775 sent a sheriff and a company of men to fill in the watercourse. A determined man, Arthur grabbed a pickaxe and threatened the men of the corporation 'using much improper language', according to a contemporary source. The dispute was settled in 1784 and he kept his free water supply.

In 1787, he responded to the influx of the new dark English style of beer and began to brew porter,

while still brewing ale. The year 1790 brought the first major expansion of the site, and in 1799 the momentous decision was taken to cease ale brewing and concentrate on porter. At the time, he made two kinds of porter: 'Town Porter' and a stronger 'Superior Porter' was born. In 1801, West India Porter was brewed, the precursor of Foreign Extra Stout. The beer was more robust than the domestic porter, as it had to withstand long sea voyages. As hops have preservative qualities, it was more heavily hopped that the domestic porter and was stronger in alcohol – both features that help its longevity and are characteristic of Foreign Extra Stout today.

Arthur Guinness died in 1803, leaving the brewery and a small fortune to his family. His son, also named Arthur, took over but initially presided over something of a slump. However, a decision to disregard costs in 1821 and go for quality led to a boom, and by 1839 output had increased to 80,000 barrels, four times the level of 1821. The use of new modes of transport – the canals

and railways – also contributed to this boom. This enabled Guinness to reach new markets in Ireland, and they employed local agents to promote their beer, and bottlers, who would then supply local markets directly.

In 1840, the brewery brewed 'Single Stout' – named because casks were marked with a single 'X' – 'Double Stout' (marked with a double 'X'), which had started life under the name Extra Superior Porter in 1821, and 'Triple Stout', the export version. Single Stout would become 'Plain Porter' in 1896 and was brewed until the 1970s. Double Stout would become 'Extra Stout' and is the excellent bottled version available today.

As the British Empire grew, so did the export trade, with Guinness 'East and West India Porter' being sold both within and beyond the Empire. Arthur Guinness II died in 1855 and his son Benjamin Lee Guinness assumed control. Under Benjamin's leadership the company grew further and this elevated the family's position in Irish society with Benjamin becoming Lord Mayor of Dublin. During this time the main features of the label that are still being used today were devised – the harp symbol, Arthur Guinness' signature and the 'Guinness' word. This was done so that no matter who the local bottler was, the beer would still bear the Guinness name.

Edward Cecil Guinness,

Benjamin's son, took over in 1868 on Benjamin's death. Under his leadership, St James's Gate would become the largest brewery in the

world. The site doubled in size and in 1873 the area between James Street and the River Liffey was acquired. Guinness now had its own quayside and therefore a direct route for exports, resulting in a fleet of barges being commissioned to transport Guinness to Dublin Port, where it was loaded onto ships. Local boys were known to gather on bridges and taunt the barge crews with shouts of 'Will ye bring us back a parrot, mister', knowing that they were only going the short distance from the Guinness quay to the port.

The brewery now covered around 60 acres and required its own narrow-gauge railway system. The brewery also had its own fire brigade. In 1886, Guinness was the first major brewery to be floated on the London Stock Exchange, with Edward Cecil becoming chairman of the company, a position held by subsequent Guinness heirs. He was given a British peerage in 1891 and established the Iveagh Trust to help the poor of Dublin and London.

Guinness employed 'travellers' who went around the pubs ostensibly to check the quality of the beer but also to assess whether the beer was being adulterated or an inferior product being passed off as Guinness. This strategy was extended worldwide in the 1890s with the appointment of overseas 'travellers'.

Back in Ireland, Guinness was tightening its grip on the market. Dublin brewers usually agreed a fixed price for selling their beer. Guinness broke these agreements on various occasions and undercut its rivals. Although profits suffered, market share increased. Many of the small country brewers gave up the struggle and became bottlers for Guinness, a trend that would continue into the twentieth century. Guinness was now available in most parts of Ireland.

The Second Earl, Rupert Guinness, assumed the chairmanship in 1927, on Edward's death. The first advertising campaign soon followed, with the advertising agency S. H. Benson employing the artist John Gilroy, who created some of the most famous and enduring Guinness images. The first campaign slogan was 'Guinness for Strength', followed by 'My Goodness, My Guinness', featuring a menagerie of zoo animals.

The 1940s saw considerable changes at the brewery, with the move to a 'sterile plant'. This mainly

meant the replacement of wooden and iron vessels with stainless-steel ones. Trials of a new draught system for Guinness began in 1958 and a year later the new draught Guinness, with the now-familiar creamy head, was launched. A large-scale advertising campaign was needed to convince punters that the newfangled keg Guinness was as good as the old cask-conditioned beer drawn from different taps. The two-stage pour was retained to bolster consumer confidence, even though the beer now came from a single keg. So successful is this form of stout dispense that all other breweries feel compelled to offer their draught stout in the same nitrogenated form.

Rupert retired as chairman in 1962, replaced by Benjamin Guinness, who would become the Third Earl Iveagh on Rupert's death in 1967. Benjamin would be the last Guinness family member to hold the chairmanship: the shareholdings of Guinness family members in the company had dwindled over the years to less than 5 percent.

As brewing became increasingly automated and comparisons were made with other less-costly breweries, it was clear that rationalisation was needed. To help with this rationalisation, the soon-to-be-notorious Ernest Saunders was recruited from Nestlé in 1981. Saunders replaced Benjamin Guinness as chairman in 1986, the first non-family member to hold the post. Control had finally left the founding family's hands though Benjamin remained on the board. However, soon afterwards, Saunders and others were convicted of fraud and other charges related to a bid for the Distillers Company and sentenced to jail terms. Benjamin died in 1992, as did Bryan Guinness, Second Baron Moyne, who was also on the board. Their deaths marked the end of the Guinness family involvement in the company, and there is no Guinness family member on the board of Diageo.

Further modernisation and automation of the brewery took place, making it one of the most technologically advanced breweries in the world. Part of the site was deemed surplus to requirements, and the brewery now covers 56 acres. The development of 'widget' technology saw the launch of Draught Guinness in a can in 1988, followed eleven years later by a bottled version. In these, a 'widget' releases nitrogen under pressure when the can or bottle is opened, mimicking the creamy head of Draught Guinness.

In 1997, Guinness merged with Grand Metropolitan to create Diageo, which has its head offices in London, and Guinness Ireland became Diageo Ireland. Guinness stout is now enjoyed in more than 150 countries around the world: it has come a long way from the small ale brewery in St James's Gate.

Availability
St James's Gate brews Guinness for Ireland, the UK, Continental Europe and the US – draught, bottled and canned. In other countries, locally brewed varieties of Guinness Foreign Extra Stout are available in bottle incorporating Guinness Flavour Extract – an evaporated hopped wort produced at St James's Gate and Diageo's Waterford plant.

Visiting
The brewery itself is not open to the public, but the Guinness Storehouse has a self-guided tour spread over many floors that shows the brewing process and other aspects of the beer, ending in the Gravity Bar with its 360° view over Dublin. The Storehouse is open daily from 9.30 till 5, with late opening until 8 in July and August.
W: www.guinness-storehouse.com
T: +353 (0)1 409 4800
EMAIL:
guinness-storehouse@guinness.com

Brewing at St James's Gate
Unfortunately Diageo were unable to provide up-to-date information regarding brewing at St James's Gate Brewery. Therefore this description of brewing may not be entirely reflective of current practice.

The brewing process takes place at two main centres: the Brewhouse for mashing and brewing and the Fermentation and Beer Processing plant for fermentation, conditioning and final processing.

The grist is made up primarily of pale malt, around 25 percent flaked barley for body and to aid head retention, and some 10 percent roasted barley for the deep, dark colour and that signature dryness. The roasted barley is made in the on-site roasthouse. Unmalted barley is heated in large drums in a similar way to how coffee-beans are roasted; indeed, the process gives the air in the vicinity of the roasthouse a roasted-coffee aroma.

The mashing regime is an upward-step infusion mash and, once completed, the wort passes through the perforated base of the mash tun, with the spent grains sold as animal feed. The wort is then boiled in the brew kettle and a number of US, German, Australian and UK hop varieties are added, such as Galena, Nugget, Goldings and Target, with possibly some hop extract.

The hopped wort is then cooled as it flows through pipes connecting the Brewhouse to the Fermentation and Beer Processing plant on the other side of James Street. After further cooling, the hopped wort is mixed with yeast and then held in huge conical fermenters for two days at around 25°C. It is claimed that a descendent of Arthur Guinness's original multi-strain yeast culture is used for fermentation, but this has now been selected down to a single strain.

Rather than rise to the top or fall to the bottom, the yeast disperses, and the green beer is clarified via a centrifuge and the yeast recovered. The green beer is pumped to the maturation tanks. In common with other large-scale brewers, Guinness practises high-gravity brewing, so the matured beer will be diluted to sales strength with highly purified water, and each batch will be blended to attain consistency in the final product. The beer is centrifuged a final time before being held in the bright beer tank ready for kegging, canning or bottling.

Guinness Flavour Extract, also called the Essence of Guinness, is made at St James's Gate as well as at Diageo's Waterford plant. A hopped wort is brewed which is then evaporated to concentrate the flavour. This is then exported to Guinness breweries worldwide. They make a standard beer from pale malt and local grains such as sorghum. The Guinness Flavour Extract is then added. The use of local grains does have an effect on the final taste: for example, the use of sorghum gives the beer an extra sourness.

Guinness recently launched the Brewhouse series in the Republic of Ireland. These are limited-edition draught stouts that taste slightly different from Draught Guinness itself. To date there have been three such brews: Brew 39, Toucan Brew and North Star Brew.

St James's Gate also makes a number of different versions of Guinness for different markets and, with St Francis Abbey Brewery in Kilkenny, brews Kilkenny ale.

DRAUGHT GUINNESS

Irish dry stout
Alcohol: 4.2%

Draught Guinness is ubiquitous in Ireland's pubs. It has a deep ruby colour with an orangey-brown creamy head. The nose is coffeeish and roasty, and has a certain earthy quality. The palate is smooth, with a latté-coffee taste and the signature roastiness. The finish has a moderate but long-lasting bitterness, a roasted dryness, and a tangy quality bordering on the sour. It is a fulsome beer and an Irish classic.

GUINNESS EXTRA STOUT

Irish dry stout
Alcohol: 4.2%

Guinness Extra Stout is the bottled version without the widget. It is an altogether different drinking experience from the nitrogenated Draught Guinness. It pours jet black with ruby highlights and a blossoming fawn head. It has a similar aroma to Draught Guinness – coffee, roast and the earthy quality – though slightly more pronounced. In the mouth it is roasty, and it has a hint of sourness which is also evident on the bitter, drying and roasty finish. Guinness Extra Stout is a beautifully assertive brew with a pronounced hoppy tang. It is probably the closest thing to how Guinness tasted before the launch of the nitrogenated Draught Guinness in the early 1960s, and is one to savour.

GUINNESS FOREIGN EXTRA STOUT

Export Irish dry stout
Alcohol: 7.5%

Guinness Foreign Extra Stout, or FES, made at St James's Gate, used to be a blended beer. Fresh stout would be blended with stout aged for around three months in old oak tuns that were around a hundred years old. During its stay in the tuns, it would be infected with the wild yeast and lactic-acid bacteria living in the tuns, giving it a musty, leathery aroma and a sour, lactic character. The sour, aged stout would be the perfect foil for the rich, young stout, ensuring that the final beer would not be too rich and cloying. After blending, it would be matured for a further month in bottle. The oak tuns are probably no longer in use, and it is not clear if this is still a blended beer.

FES is almost jet black in colour, with a dense orange-brown foam. The nose is so complex that it is hard to know where to start when it comes to describing it. There are aromas of coffee, dark fruit and roasted grain, with a possible hint of musty leather from the wild yeast. The beer is rich, assertive, oily and full bodied in the mouth, and the finish is drying, with notes of burnt currants, espresso coffee and sour fruit, and an intense, long-lasting bitterness. This beer can accompany the richest desserts but is probably best as an after-dinner drink or nightcap. It may or may not be made in the traditional way, but the St James's Gate FES remains a classic beer, rich, fully-flavoured and supremely complex: the ultimate Guinness.

HARP LAGER/ GREAT NORTHERN BREWERY

Carrick Road, Dundalk, County Louth
T: +353 (0)1 453 6700
(Diageo Ireland)
W: www.diageo.ie

The Great Northern Brewery is the second-largest brewery in Ireland, the largest being St James's Gate in Dublin. It is, also like St James's Gate, owned by the drinks multinational Diageo and is best known for being the home of Harp Lager.

However, the history of the brewery long predates Harp Lager. It was founded in 1897 by directors of the Great Northern Railway Company with a capital sum of £30,000. The brewery was aptly named the Great Northern Brewery and located opposite Dundalk railway station on the Dublin to Belfast main line. The brewery made three products: a light dessert ale, a highly popular amber ale and a strong ale, reported to be a very potent brew indeed.

The Great Northern Brewery continued to brew ale and porter until it was bought by Smithwick's of Kilkenny in 1953. Smithwick's were enjoying great success with their No. 1 Ale and looking to increase capacity, as they had become a company with national, rather than regional, distribution. However, a bacteriological infection at their Kilkenny brewery provided the impetus for modernisation. The greater brewing capacity of the modernised brewery in Kilkenny meant that the Great Northern Brewery became surplus to requirements and was only being used for malting.

In 1957, Smithwick's leased the brewery to a Guinness-led consortium, eventually selling it to them in 1960. Guinness had decided to get into the lager market, and a consortium was established in which they had 50 percent of the shares, the remaining shares being owned by a number of British brewers. The Great Northern Brewery was seen as the perfect location not only due to its rail links to Dublin and Belfast – two key markets – but also thanks to the character of the local water supply. This water, from the Ravensdale Reservoir in the Cooley Mountains, was said to be similar to that of the great lager-brewing areas in the Czech Republic.

Work began on the site in 1959, resulting in the demolition of much of the old brewery, though some of the Victorian architecture was retained, to construct a brand-new lager brewery, at a cost of £2 million. It was renamed the Harp Lager Brewery.

Dr Herman Muender was

recruited to oversee production. Dr Muender was a German national who had made his name by being involved in the reconstruction of German breweries following the Second World War. Brewing started in 1960, and 6,000 barrels were sold. It soon became apparent that the plant would not be able to cope with the demand – sales having shot up to 50,000 barrels only two years later – so more money was invested to extend brewing capacity.

The phenomenal growth continued: the 100,000-barrel mark was reached in 1966, and in 1971 sales hit 250,000 barrels. However, in 1978 the consortium collapsed as Scottish and Newcastle, and Courage, withdrew, having developed their own lagers: Hoffmeister and McEwan's respectively. A new company was set up – Harp Limited – with shares owned by Guinness, Greene King, and Wolverhampton and Dudley. During this time, in 1982, sales reached 500,000 barrels. Wolverhampton and Dudley left in 1985 and the Harp Lager Company came into being, with 75 percent of the shares in Guinness hands and the remainder with Greene King. Following the withdrawal of Greene King in 1990 the company was 100 percent Guinness owned, and is now therefore part of Diageo.

By this time the brewery was producing a number of other lagers, such as Steiger, Satzenbrau and the alcohol-free Kaliber. Kaliber was brewed in the same way as Harp before having the alcohol removed. In the late 1980s, these beers were joined by Carlsberg, as the contract for brewing it under licence passed from Beamish and Crawford to the Harp Lager Brewery.

As well as lager, the brewery also brews some ale. In 2001, Diageo closed Dundalk's other brewery, Macardle Moore, transferring the production of Macardles Ale to the Harp Lager Brewery. The brewery also brews some Smithwick's Ale, which is fitting, considering its past. The brewery is connected to its past in another way: it has recently been renamed the Great Northern Brewery.

Availability

Harp is available in many countries throughout the world, some of which brew the beer at local breweries under licence. Satzenbrau is mainly available in Ireland. Macardles Ale has a limited availability in Ireland and is easiest to find around Dundalk.

Visiting

The Great Northern Brewery is not open to the public.

Brewing

Unfortunately Diageo were unable to provide up to date information regarding brewing at the Great Northern Brewery. Therefore this description of brewing may not be entirely reflective of current practice.

Harp follows a decoction mashing regime. A third of the mash is separated away and heated up in steps to boiling point. This is then returned to the main mash, bringing it up to 70°C. Decoction mashing is widely used in continental lager brewing but mainly due to the low quality of continental barley. This regime was instituted at the Great Northern Brewery by Dr Muender, no doubt due to his German brewing heritage. Irish barley does not generally suffer the same quality problems as continental varieties and therefore does not necessarily require a decoction mashing regime.

The wort is filtered in a lauter tun before being boiled for 90 minutes. The hopped wort is cooled to 10°C for fermentation. It is fermented using a lager yeast that was originally from a Bavarian brewery. After fermentation is complete and the yeast is cropped, or removed, and the green beer is lagered at below 0°C for approximately one month. It is then filtered en route to the bright beer tank in which carbonation is adjusted and it is then ready to be packaged.

HARP

Standard lager
Alcohol: 4.0%

Harp lager is the flagship brand that has proven very successful. The grist is lager malt and it is hopped with Czech and German varieties. It pours a light gold colour offering very little on the nose, possibly some hints of malt and citrus. The palate is clean and the finish is short with a very light hop bitterness. Harp is a simple refreshing lager that belongs to the inoffensive mainstream and thus lacks any depth and has little to offer in the way of flavour.

SATZENBRAU PREMIUM PILS

European-style Pilsner
Alcohol: 5.0%

Although Satzenbrau has a Germanic sounding name, it is actually a beer developed at the Great Northern Brewery. 'Satz', as it is known, is golden in colour with muted floral and grassy notes on the nose. There is a hint of spiciness in the mouth and the finish is characterised by a light hop bitterness. Although it is described as a genuine pils (or pilsner) it is not robustly flavoured enough to live up to its claim and has a certain harshness that diminishes its appeal.

MACARDLES

Irish red ale
Alcohol: 4.0%

Macardles ale is a reminder of Dundalk's brewing past. Macardle Moore was a brewery based just over the road from the Great Northern Brewery on the other side of the railway line. The company was formed in 1863 and based at Cambricville. This was the site of the Stuart Brewery since at least 1704 though it had closed in by 1854. British brewer Ind Coope took a significant interest in the company in the 1950s and it began to brew its Double Diamond Ale. In 1961 Macardle Moore became part of the newly-formed Irish Ale Breweries in which Guinness had a large share. It passed fully into Guinness hands in 1988 when Irish Ale Breweries was dissolved and was closed by Diageo in 2001.

Macardles is made with pale malt, roasted barley for colour and flaked maize for head retention. It has a standard infusion mash for 90 minutes at around 65°C before being hopped with three bittering hop varieties and one aroma hop. Macardles is a deep amber colour with a malty, toasty and nutty aroma and flavour. The finish has the appropriate light bitterness of the style. Macardles is a very enjoyable ale and without a doubt the pick of the ales made by Diageo in Ireland, it is a shame that it is not more widely available.

Heineken Ireland

Murphy Brewery, Leitrim Street, Cork
T: +353 (0)21 450 3371
W: www.heinekenireland.com
E: HIinfo@heineken.ie

Until 2001 Heineken Ireland was known as Murphy's. The brewery, on Cork's north side, was founded in 1856 by James J Murphy and his brothers and was known as James J Murphy & Company. James J was the senior partner in the business, hailing from a wealthy and distinguished Catholic family. He had numerous business interests, including shares in the Murphy's Whiskey Distillery in Midleton, and was well-known for charitable work.

They chose the site of the former Cork Foundling Hospital and invested a large sum to turn it into a brewery which was named Lady's Well after a holy well nearby. Initially there were two beers brewed – Murphy's Porter and Lady's Well Ale.

Although the ale was discontinued in 1861, the brewery prospered and built up an estate of tied public houses. It quickly became one of the big Cork brewers, helped in this by being run by a Catholic family which distinguished it from Beamish and Crawford and Guinness, as these were both owned by Protestant families.

In the 1880s the brewery was given a major renovation, which included the building of the impressive maltings that now houses the offices of Heineken Ireland. Murphy's Stout was brewed for the first time at the end of this decade in 1889.

The brewery became a limited company on 31 December 1883 with the shares owned by Murphy family members. James J. Murphy died in 1897 and from then on the shares began to diffuse into the

extended family.

In 1901 Arnotts Brewery in Cork was purchased. It had been one of Cork's major breweries but went into decline following the death of Sir John Arnott. It was not the brewery as such that was of interest to Murphy's, but its estate of tied houses. The brewery was closed and the tied houses were subsumed into the Murphy's estate.

By the time the company celebrated fifty years of brewing, it had grown to be the largest brewery in Ireland after Guinness with an output of 125,000 barrels. One interesting image from this time depicted Eugene Sandow, a famous strongman, holding up a horse and endorsing Murphy's Stout. This was an enduring feature of Murphy's advertising until the second half of the twentieth century and predated the later 'Guinness for strength' campaign by about forty years.

In the 1910s, the process of replacing old wooden vessels with aluminium ones began, but was cut short by the First World War. It would be finally completed in 1951. During the war Murphy's, like their counterparts Beamish and Guinness, supplied British Army barracks in what was a fairly lucrative trade.

The War of Independence and the following Civil War that followed brought severe disruption. This was felt keenly by Murphy's as military activity was strongest in the south, where Murphy's had most of their trade, and their export trade was limited. Furthermore, general economic conditions throughout the 1920s and 1930s were poor and output fell into steady decline. By 1924 output had fallen to 60,000 barrels, half the pre-First World War level, hitting a low in 1935 when output sunk to 23,000 barrels.

The brewery worker's strike in 1920 enabled Guinness to gain a foothold in Cork – they had been previously kept at bay thanks to the tied house system. As the strike also affected Beamish and Crawford, publicans turned to Guinness to supply the beer. A move that would have far-reaching effects as Guinness never relinquished this foothold.

When Guinness switched to metal kegs in the early 1960s and a nitrogenated product instead of cask-conditioned stout, lack of investment over the years meant that Murphy's was not in a position to do likewise. However, they attempted to capitalise on consumer doubts about draught stout with the slogan – 'Murphy's from the wood, that's good'.

However in 1967 they did eventually follow suit.

The 1950s saw a period of decline. Lack of investment in the

plant also brought problems with quality and some loss of trade with Guinness being the main beneficiary. Guinness approached Murphy's in 1960, looking to eliminate another competitor by taking over the brewery, but this approach was rebuffed.

In the 1960s ale and lager were gaining an increasing share in the beer market. The fact that Murphy's brewed neither led to a partnership with British brewer Watney Mann, who bought a 30 percent share in Murphy's. Murphy's now sold Watney's Red Barrel ale which was an initial success. The partnership also meant sales of Murphy's stout throughout the Watney Mann and Bass Charrington tied estates in Britain. In 1967 Watney Mann acquired 51 percent of the shares and overall control of the company left the hands of the Murphy family.

However, by the early 1970s Watney Mann were beginning to lose interest as sales declined and they were also experiencing problems in their home market. As no buyers came forward for their shares, they petitioned for the company to be wound up. At the very last moment Taoiseach Jack Lynch, whose constituency included the Murphy's brewery, intervened and the Watney Mann share was bought by the state rescue service, Taiscí Stáit Teoranta, later to become Fóir Teoranta.

Losses grew in the early 1970s. In 1974, the Licensed Vintners Cooperative Society – made up of one thousand publicans – bought just under 50 percent of the shares. Initially the brewery did well under the new ownership and the Cooperative bought the remaining shares, renaming the company Murphy's Brewery Ltd. Ownership had now passed from the Murphy family although Lt Col John F. Murphy – grandson of James J. – was made Honorary Life President. The 1970s also saw the beginning of the end of the tied estate, which were becoming expensive to maintain.

Throughout the 1970s, ale and lager continued to grow in popularity. Murphy's tried a few different English and Scottish ales but with no great success. They then approached Heineken to brew its lager under licence. Initially Heineken were not enthusiastic but when the product was given its Irish launch in 1978 it performed very well. However, the brewery was again struggling and Heineken were asked to take a direct

shareholding. They refused and subsequent negotiations, with Beamish and Crawford to take over the brewery also failed after the deal was rejected by Murphy's shareholders.

On 23 September 1980, Lt Col John F Murphy died – he was the last of the family to have a direct involvement in the brewery. Unfortunately, at this time the brewery was in bad shape, and it went into receivership in 1982. By now, Heineken had created a substantial market share for itself and was reluctant to abandon it. After negotiations they secured some assistance from the Industrial Development Authority and Fóir Teoranta and Murphy's Brewery Ireland Ltd became a wholly owned subsidiary of Heineken on 1 April 1983.

Since the Heineken takeover the brewery has received massive investment. This led to the demolition of the old brewhouse with its 199-foot chimney, a long-time feature of the Cork skyline. This was replaced by a new brewhouse with the latest technology. The brewery has experienced sustained growth and in 2001 the name was changed to

Heineken Ireland. The brewery has since gone from strength to strength and the future looks bright indeed for this Cork brewery.

Availability
Murphy's Stout is available throughout Ireland and in seventy countries worldwide.

Visiting
The brewery is not open to the public.

Brewing Murphy's Stout

The brewery has an output of around 800,000 hectolitres a year with Murphy's Stout making up around 20 percent of that total. The brewery operates twenty-four hours, five days a week and can brew around 320 hectolitres per batch.

The malt is sourced locally from the Malting Company of Ireland in Cork and from Irish Malt Exports in the Midlands. The grain silos lie on the other side of Leitrim Street to the remainder of the plant and makes its way to the mash tuns via a conveyor that bridges the road. Mains water is used for brewing liquor. It is treated on site to ensure that it has all the prerequisite characteristics of brewing liquor.

Mashing lasts ninety minutes, starting at around 50°C and proceeds upwards in a series of steps to 70°C. The wort is then pumped to a lauter tun for clarification. The boil also lasts ninety minutes where the wort is hopped with a mixture of pellets and hop extract. A whirlpool separates the hopped wort from any remaining residue which, together with spent grains from the lauter tun, is sold to farmers for animal feed.

The hopped wort is cooled to 20°C in preparation for fermentation. Fermentation takes place in large closed conical fermenters using the original Murphy's yeast which is renewed every six generations. It usually lasts just over two days at 18-20°C and the brewery practices high gravity brewing, so the final alcohol content will be roughly twice the content of the beer when sold. The yeast is single-strain and flocculent, so that when fermentation is complete and the tanks are cooled to 10°C for conditioning, the yeast clumps together and falls to the bottom where it is removed.

The green beer remains in the same tank in which fermentation took place but with the yeast removed. Conditioning lasts six to eight days at 10°C. The beer is then chilled to around 0°C and centrifuged, after which it is diluted with highly purified water down to the sales alcohol level. The beer is carbonated and nitrogenated prior to kegging and the kegs are flash pasteurised. Canning is done elsewhere.

There are quality-control checks at each stage, with daily taste tests of the water and malt. The beer itself is always tasted at 9.30 am.

As well as Murphy's Stout the brewery also brews Heineken, Coors Light and Amstel lagers.

MURPHY'S STOUT

Irish dry stout
Alcohol: 4.0%

Murphy's Stout is brewed with around 90 percent pale malt with the remainder being a blend of roasted barley and chocolate malt. Target hops are added in pellet form at the beginning of the boil together with hop extract. There is no late hopping.

The stout has a creamy white head and is a deep ruby colour but not fully opaque. It has a delicate roastiness on the nose with a background hint of chocolate. It is fairly light in the mouth with more roastiness and a little touch of sweetness. The finish has a delicate but lingering hop bitterness and grain roastiness with a taste reminiscent of currants, producing in Murphy's one of the milder interpretations of Irish dry stout.

HILDEN BREWERY

**Grand Street,
Hilden, Lisburn,
Co. Antrim, BT27 4TY
Tel: +44 (0)2892 660800
W: www.hildenbrewery.co.uk
E: irishbeers@hildenbrewery.co.uk**

Hilden is a craft brewery located in the village of the same name between the cities of Belfast and Lisburn. The brewery is the oldest craft brewery in Ireland and was founded in 1981 by Seamus and Ann Scullion, at a time when many British microbreweries were also taking their first steps. The pair lived in England for a while and developed a taste for cask-conditioned ale. They saw that the choice of beer in English pubs was far greater than that in Northern Ireland. They decided to move back home and set up in business to increase choice for the Northern Ireland beer-drinker. Hilden Brewery was born.

The brewery itself is situated in a cobbled courtyard behind a large house that once belonged to the prosperous owner of Barbour Threads linen mill. The imposing remains of the mill can be found a short distance away behind the brewery. The house, courtyard and outbuildings date from the early 1800s and the brewery occupies one side of the courtyard's whitewashed former stables.

Occupying another side of the courtyard is the Tap Room Restaurant. Opened in 1995, it not only has a reputation for excellent food, but is also a great place to sample Hilden's ales. Hilden Brewery also organise a very popular beer festival in the courtyard on the August bank holiday weekend.

Throughout its history, Hilden has experienced fluctuating fortunes. Initially, they were successful in getting the bars of Northern Ireland to stock their beer. However, the number of outlets slowly declined over time. This is largely attributed to the fact that the supply of beer to the pubs of Northern Ireland is in the hands of a Bass (Inbev) and Guinness (Diageo) duopoly. To make up for the declining sales in Northern Ireland, Hilden have been selling their cask-conditioned ale directly to pubs and clubs in Scotland and northern England.

However, the future looks bright. The company is currently looking to target Northern Ireland again with a renewed vigour. They are working to increase the number of pubs selling the beer and to expand the bottled range for the off-trade.

Availability

As well as being served in the Tap Room Restaurant, Hilden's ales are available on draught in Belfast's John Hewitt Bar, and there are plans to increase the number of local outlets in the near future. They are also available in the pubs and clubs of Scotland's central belt as well as in pubs in the English counties of Staffordshire, Cheshire and Lancashire. Hilden's ales can also be found at major regional English beer festivals. In addition, a bottled range is about to be relaunched; this should make the company's ales more widely available.

Tours

Brewery tours are run Monday to Friday at 11.30 am and 5 pm but it is advisable to check in advance. The tour includes a look inside the brewhouse, an explanation of the brewing process and a free pint of your choice at the bar.

HILDEN BREWERY

Brewing at Hilden

The current head brewer is Owen Scullion, Ann and Seamus's son. He is passionate about cask-conditioned ale, having grown up with beer at Hilden, and is a graduate of the Institute of Brewing and Distilling at Heriot-Watt University near Edinburgh. Before moving back to run the family business, he spent seven years in Scotland working with brewers Bellhaven and Scottish Courage.

The brewhouse is small and compact, with an output capacity of 35 hectolitres. All the equipment is stainless steel and was made locally. On average, Hilden brews once a week and the output is evenly distributed among the five products.

The brewing liquor is drawn from the public water supply, although there are plans to use a borehole in the near future. Untreated, it is soft and used for Silver pale ale and Molly Malone Porter. For Hilden Ale, Hilden Halt and Scullion's Irish the water is burtonised. The malt and hops come from England. Hilden use only whole-cone hops and concentrate on English hop varieties

such as Challenger, First Gold, Goldings and Northdown, with the Czech Saaz hop used in its Silver pale ale.

Brewing at Hilden is done in a very traditional way, and all of the ales are brewed in the same way. It starts with a 65°C infusion mash lasting for an hour and a half. The only adjunct is wheat flour to help with head retention in the final beer. The wort is then pumped to the stainless-steel, direct-fired brew kettle, where it boils for an hour and ten minutes. The brew kettle is only half the size of the other equipment, so Hilden have to brew twice to reach their full output.

Before passing through the heat exchanger, the hopped wort cools in the hop back for forty-five minutes, at which point further hops are added for Scullion's Irish. The hop back has a perforated base and strains the hopped wort, leaving behind the hope cones and other residue as it makes its way to fermentation.

The fermentation is of the traditional open variety, and the hopped wort is pitched with a single-strain brewer's yeast. Fermentation

happens at around 18-20°C and lasts for four days. After two days of cooling, the green beer is put into casks or bottles, where it matures, or conditions, for a week to ten days after being primed with a little more yeast and fined with Isinglass. It is not filtered or pasteurised.

Hilden Brewery makes five different beers, each one available in cask form, with a certain nuttiness coming through as the house style. The bottled range is about to be relaunched.

HILDEN ALE
English-style bitter
Alcohol: 4.0%

The brewery's original ale is an easy-drinking traditional bitter, where pale ale malt is joined by crystal and chocolate malts for character and colour. Hilden Ale is hopped with Northdown, Goldings and First Gold for bitterness, with a late addition of Goldings for aroma and flavour.

It pours a darkish amber colour with a sweetish, malty, complex nose

Owen Scullion at the brew kettle

boil and in the hop back.

A slightly darker shade of amber than Hilden Ale, almost tawny. There are nuts and sweet floral hops on the nose, with more nuts and juicy malt on the palate. The finish is gently mouth-drying, with some clean, lingering hop bitterness, making for a refreshing ale that would pair well with sweet meats such as pork.

HILDEN HALT

Strong ale
Alcohol: 4.6%

A newcomer to the Hilden family, named after the local railway station. A significant quantity of crystal malt is used for colour, with a small quantity of black malt and the usual pale ale malt. Progress, Challenger and First Gold are the bittering hops, with Styrian Goldings added at the end of the boil for flavour and aroma.

Hilden Halt is a deep tawny coloured beer with a treacle, nutty, even vinous nose, with hints of spice in the background. The palate is rich and malty, with that hint of spice still in the background – and remaining in the malty finish. This is a richly flavoured strong ale that would be a match for strongly flavoured foods such as stews and casseroles.

of culinary apple, and earthy hops with hints of strawberry. On the palate the main characteristic is nuttiness, and the finish is long, bitter and drying. A pleasant, enjoyable ale and a good introduction to Hilden's house style.

SCULLION'S IRISH

Irish ale
Alcohol: 4.6%

Named after the family, this is not quite an Irish red ale. Rather it is something in between a traditional Irish red ale and an English style bitter. The malts are the same as for Hilden Ale: pale ale, crystal and chocolate. However, the hopping differs: Goldings, First Gold and Challenger are the bittering hops, with Progress added at the end of the

SILVER
Pale ale
Alcohol: 4.2%

Although technically a pale ale, Silver is really brewed to be a lager and was devised to satisfy the lager drinkers at the Tap Room Restaurant. However, with the advent of Belfast Blonde, made for Hilden's sister brewery – College Green – Silver will become a fully fledged pale ale in the future.

Lager malt makes up nearly the whole of the mash, with a touch of crystal malt to darken the final beer fractionally. There is no late hopping, but First Gold and Challenger are joined by the classic lager hop Saaz at the beginning of the boil.

Light gold in colour, with a floral hop aroma and notes of candied orange. The biscuity malt comes through more on the palate, as does orange and that certain Hilden nuttiness. The finish has citric fruit and some light hop bitterness. As it is currently brewed as a lager, it lacks the more robust hop bitterness of a true pale ale. It is nevertheless a very pleasant beer and, as it morphs into a true pale ale, it could be one to watch out for.

Unlike Hilden's other beers, which are drawn by handpump, this is served carbonated, with mixed gas further to resemble lager. Again, this will change when it becomes a pale ale.

MOLLY MALONE
Porter
Alcohol: 4.6%

Owen Scullion isn't a fan of this slightly gimmicky name, but behind it is an interesting story. The Hogs Head chain of pubs in Great Britain used to specialise in real ale. For the Five (as it was then) Nations Rugby Union Championship, it was decided that each country would be represented by a beer. Hogs Head's owners Whitbread commissioned Hilden to brew a porter to be Ireland's representative and provided the name Molly Malone.

The mash is pale ale, chocolate and black malt. Challenger hops provide the bitterness, and Goldings the flavour, with First Gold again providing both bitterness and flavour.

Molly Malone is almost black, with very dark amber highlights. It has a lovely roasty, coffee and dark-fruit nose, with more roastedness and dark fruit on the palate. The finish has a firm bitterness and a good length. Molly Malone is a fine example of porter, not as bitter or full-bodied as a stout but with greater fruitiness, making it a good match for fruity desserts.

Aidan Murphy

HOOKER BREWERY

**Roscommon Business Park,
Racecourse Road,
Roscommon Town
W: www.galwayhooker.ie
E: info@galwayhooker.ie**

Cousins Aidan Murphy and Ronan Brennan are the people behind one of the newest beers in Ireland. Aidan had spent some time working in a brewpub in San Francisco and when he moved back to Ireland the first wave of craft brewing was underway, sparking his interest to set one up himself. He then studied brewing at Heriot-Watt and worked in a brewery on the Isle of Man. In 2005 he and Ronan, who has a background in hotel management, decided they would give it a go and looked around for a brewery. They found one in Roscommon town: the Emerald Brewery.

This brewery was part of the first wave of craft brewing but did not survive very long. It brewed and bottled a lager called Emerald Gold in 1999 but ceased production soon after. Indeed when Aidan and Ronan first saw the brewery it was like the Marie Celeste – half-full bottles were still in the bottler and paperwork was still on the desk. Nobody had been there in six years.

They secured some initial funding, but before committing capital to leasing the brewery, they needed to prove that there was a market for a craft beer in Galway and so had the beer contract brewed by Biddy Early in County Clare. Galway Hooker was launched in the summer of 2006 in eight pubs in Galway city, selected as they were thought to have customers who were most likely to try a new product.

... We thought you'd like something different

Galway
hooker
IRISH PALE ALE

Sales are improving and the beer has developed a following. The number of outlets is increasing and they hope to be brewing in Galway in the near future.

They seem to be well on their way to achieving their goal of giving the people of Galway back a pint of the local stuff.

Availability
The beer is available on draught in over ten pubs in Galway city.

Visiting
As they have only started to brew in Roscommon, opening the brewery to the public is not a priority. However, it may be possible to visit the brewery but anyone interested must contact them in advance.

Brewing the Hooker
The Hooker Brewery is an industrial unit on a business park in Roscommon town. The brew length is between six and seven hectolitres and that is sufficient for current requirements. Having only two fermenters means that brewing cannot be done more than twice a week.

The local mains water is hard and it is burtonised for brewing liquor. Hooker get all their malt from England as Irish maltsters do not cater for very small operations such as this one. The mash tun is direct-fired and mashing lasts around one hour at 64°C. The wort is clarified by circulating it over the mash before going to the brew kettle.

Pellet hops are used and are added to the wort during the one hour boil.

The hopped wort is clarified by being put through a whirlpool before passing through a heat exchanger for cooling down to around 17°C.

The fermenting vessels are closed conicals and the hopped wort is pitched with the Chico yeast strain from the Sierra Nevada Brewery in the US. Fermentation happens at around 21°C and lasts four to five days. The green beer is then conditioned in tanks at 1°C in the cold store for three weeks. The beer is then filtered before being kegged from the bright beer tank after adjusting carbonation. The beer is delivered fresh, without pasteurisation or preservatives, similar to how local breweries would have done in the past.

GALWAY HOOKER

Pale ale
Alcohol: 4.4%

Aidan and Ronan could not decide what to call their new beer. As all of their friends had a different opinion, they thought of an innovative way to launch the beer and generate some interest. A website was set up where people could suggest names. The suggestions were shortlisted and people were invited to vote on the final name – Galway Hooker emerged as the winner. The beer is named after a traditional sailing craft of Galway Bay but has other connotations which are played upon in advertising, with slogans such as 'nothing goes down like a Galway Hooker'.

A pale ale was chosen because Aidan is a fan of the style and they wanted to do a niche beer style that was not being produced by one of the major brewers. Pale malt dominates the grist with some crystal for colour and character and wheat malt for head retention. There are three hop additions. First Gold and Fuggles are added at the start of the boil. Then, unusually for a pale ale, Saaz is added just before boil end, followed by a more conventional late addition of the US Cascade hop for its signature fruitiness.

Galway Hooker is a tawny-copper colour and has a wonderfully complex nose of citrus, especially grapefruit, and resiny hops balanced against biscuity sweetness from the malt. More grapefruit and citrus in the mouth with a robust, refreshing bitterness in the finish, characterised by peppery hops that turn citric as the finish develops. This is an excellent example of a pale ale; very complex and well-balanced, fully flavoured with a great finish making it a highly refreshing and more-ish beer. A great apéritif but the citrussy nature also makes it a good match for spicy Mexican and oriental food.

KINSALE BREWING COMPANY

**The Glen, Kinsale,
County Cork
T: +353 (0)21 470 2124
W: www.kinsalebrewing.com
E: info@kinsalebrewing.com**

Kinsale is a beautiful harbour town on the south coast of Ireland and tourist hotspot during the summer. There is over three hundred years of brewing tradition at Kinsale and the current brewery stands on the site of the Landers brewery, which dates from 1703. It became the Williams brewery in the 1800s before falling into disuse, one of the many small brewers that disappeared throughout Ireland. When the Kiley brothers acquired the site, it was a coal yard.

The Kiley brothers, Barry, Albert and Cathal, had been impressed by the brewpubs of New York and thought that it was time to challenge the dominance of the big brewers in Ireland. They also thought that the Irish-American community in the US would be interested in Irish craft brews and looked to export there from an early stage.

Kinsale Irish Lager was launched in 1998 and brewed under contract by Beamish and Crawford up the road in Cork. The beer was well supported around Kinsale with many pubs stocking it on draught. The present brewhouse is found through an archway behind a whitewashed exterior and brewing began there in 2001. With the new brewhouse up and running, the range of beers was increased and these are also beginning to get into the bars of the town. As well as a brewery, there is also a bar and a shop on the site, both open to the general public. The Kiley brothers are now branching into the bottled market, with three of the range currently being packaged as bottle conditioned beers.

Kinsale Irish Lager is widely available in the town of Kinsale and other towns in the locality. It can also be found in Galway and is imported into the US by Cavalier Distribution of Ohio. The other four beers can be found in Kinsale and the bottles will be available in selected off-licences as well as the Carry Out, Londis and Supervalu supermarket chains.

Visiting

Tours run at 4 pm Tuesday to Saturday from May to the end of September. Visitors will get an insight into the history of Kinsale as well as a tour around the brewery and a description of the brewing process. The tour ends with a complimentary drink in the bar. There is also a shop on the site selling Kinsale Brewery merchandise.

Brewing in Kinsale

The glass-fronted, compact brewhouse has an output of around 180 hectolitres a year, well below its capacity as it can produce around 10 hectolitres per brew. Output is now on the increase following the decision to start bottling some of its range. The brewery brews four beers whilst Kinsale Irish Lager – the mainstay of the business – continues to be made by Beamish and Crawford, as the yearly production of two thousand hectolitres is too big for the brewery at Kinsale to handle.

The master brewer is Englishman David Pickering, who holds a brewing diploma from Heriot-Watt University and used to brew in Leeds at one of the Firkin chain of brewpubs. He met his girlfriend whilst brewing in New Zealand and moved to Ireland, getting a job at the Kinsale Brewing Company. David usually brews once a week in winter and three times a week in summer, with output divided fairly evenly among the four beers.

The equipment is German-built but came to Kinsale the long way round, having seen service in a brewpub in Singapore. The brewing liquor, which comes from the municipal water supply, is soft in character but is burtonised to specification. David uses an upward-step infusion mash so that Williams Wheat and 1703 Lager start in the low 50s before being raised to 66°C and then a final step to 77°C. Cream Stout and Landers Ale have a slightly simpler mashing regime as they skip the first step and start at 66°C.

The mash is pumped to a lauter tun for clarification and then returns to the mash tun which now becomes the brew kettle. 1703 is boiled for an hour whilst the other beers get seventy-five minutes, during which pelletised hops are added. The hopped wort is clarified via a whirlpool before passing through a heat exchanger to cool for fermentation. 1703 ferments at 12°C for two weeks whilst the other beers ferment at 20°C for five days. All

David Pickering

fermentation is open except for Williams Wheat, which has a closed fermentation under pressure. Kinsale use two single strain yeasts, a lager yeast for 1703 and a vigorous brewers yeast for the other beers.

Cool water flowing in jackets around the fermentation vessel keep the temperature under control and then cools the green beer to around 5°C before it makes the trip to the conditioning tanks in the cold store. The beers will condition for a week with the exception of 1703, which receives three to four weeks conditioning.

After adjusting the carbonation, Williams Wheat is kegged straight from the conditioning tank, whilst the other beers are filtered before the carbonation is adjusted in the bright beer tank.

Seasonal specialities are planned. Christmas will feature a strong 7.5 percent alcohol winter warmer, while there will be a Belgian saison-style beer for the spring, a fruity wheat beer in the summer and an amber ale for autumn.

KINSALE IRISH LAGER

German-style pilsner
Alcohol: 4.3%

The flagship beer and only available on draught. The grist is mainly pale malt with caramalt for body and a touch of malted wheat to aid head retention. The hopping is very traditional for this style of beer – Perle for bittering and Saaz for a noble aroma and flavour. The beer is pasteurised as it is exported as well as consumed in the domestic market.

Light gold in colour with a creamy white head, it has a very delicate nose with hints of grassiness, spice and honey. In the mouth it is crisp with a slight tanginess. This is followed by a short but clean and refreshing finish with light hop bitterness. This is a delicate, simple, clean lager that skirts close to the inoffensive mainstream rather than being a true German-style pilsner.

KINSALE 1703

Czech-style pilsner
Alcohol: 5.9%

The year 1703 was the founding date of the original brewery on the site occupied by Kinsale Brewing. Pale malt makes up 95 percent of the grist, with the balance being caramalt. There are four hop additions which aim to set 1703 apart from other lagers – Perle at the start and half an hour into the boil, then Saaz is added at the forty-five minute mark and again at the end.

1703 is fuller gold in colour than Kinsale Irish Lager, with good flowery aromas from the Saaz hop and some toasted malt, pine and grassy notes. A spicy, tangy, almost woody palate is followed by a dry and delicate hop bitterness in the finish. 1703 is a delicate interpretation of a Czech pilsner but enjoys a fuller flavour than Kinsale Irish Lager.

Kinsale 1703 is also available as a bottle-conditioned beer, which is slightly lower in alcohol, at 5.6 percent.

WILLIAMS WHEAT BEER

Belgian-style wheat beer
Alcohol: 4.3%

Named after the Williams family who owned the predecessor brewery in the 1800s, this beer has a high quantity of wheat malt, 60 percent, together with 35 percent pale malt and 5 percent crystal malt for sweetness. The Brewers Gold hop is added both at the start and the end of the boil, with Perle joining it at the end to balance the sweetness. Also added at the end of the boil are some orange peel and coriander to give it the authentic Belgian wheat beer characteristics.

Williams Wheat pours with a fluffy white head and a hazy straw-coloured body. There is a very fragrant, citrussy nose of oranges and lemons with spicy notes also coming into play. More oranges follow on the palate which also has a good degree of tartness. The finish is quenching, slightly tangy and has a nice crisp acidity. Williams Wheat is a great beer full of good strong flavours and could pair well with shellfish or stand up to salads made with strong vinaigrette.

LANDERS ALE

English-style bitter
Alcohol: 4.3%

Landers Ale is named in honour of the first family to brew in Kinsale back in 1703. Rather than do an Irish red ale, the thinking here was to do something different in order to stand out from the crowd and so something approaching an extra special bitter was brewed. Pale ale malt is 80 percent of the grist, while there is 15 percent caramalt for body; the rest is made up mainly of crystal malt with a touch of chocolate malt for colour.

Dark copper in colour with an off-white head, there is strong orange marmalade on the nose joined by some roastiness and creamy toffee. More citric fruit follows in the mouth and a hint of nuttiness. The finish is tangy, citric and drying with a nice lingering bitterness. Landers is a lovely and refreshing ale that would go well with light sweet meets such as pork.

The bottle-conditioned version is stronger in alcohol at 5.6 percent and more assertively hoppy.

KINSALE CREAM STOUT

Sweet stout
Alcohol 4.3%

Rather than do the usual dry stout, Kinsale have again done something a little different by producing a sweet stout, though not as sweet as some, such as the English Mackeson. Pale malt accounts for 70 percent of the grist with 20 percent being caramalt. Chocolate malt makes up the majority of the remainder with a touch of roasted barley. Kinsale Cream Stout is hopped with First Gold for bitterness and Perle at boil end.

Kinsale Cream Stout is jet black with a creamy coloured head. A complex nose reveals smokey, woody, oaky hints with a delicate roastiness and nutty notes. There is sweetness on the palate but not overly so, and there is also some burnt caramel. The finish is smoky but not bitter. This is a very interesting and well-balanced stout with a nice level of sweetness, something a bit different to all other Irish brewed stouts. Being sweet, it could partner chocolate and creamy desserts such as chocolate cheesecake.

On draught it is nitrogenated, a bottle-conditioned version is also available, stronger in alcohol at 5.6 percent.

MESSRS MAGUIRES

1 & 2 Burgh Quay, Dublin 2
☎: +353 (0)1 670 5777

Messrs Maguires brewpub sits on the Liffey near O'Connell Bridge in the heart of Dublin. The building it occupies is nearly two hundred years old and was originally owned by a Captain James Connolly. Number one Burgh Quay was a tavern, whilst number two's original leaseholders were the Dublin Library Society. In the 1830s, number two had come into the hands of the Maguires, who were ropemakers, and number one was known as the Corn Exchange Tavern.

History also suggests that there was once a small brewery on Burgh Quay, but it was demolished by order of the Wide Streets Commission and the Corn Exchange now stands on the site.

The initial groundswell of brewpubs in Ireland – Biddy Early, Porterhouse, Dwan's – made many people think this was a trend that was about to take off. On the back of this trend, developer Sean Quinn set up Messrs Maguires brewpub in 1998. Although it has not developed to the same extent as the Porterhouse, it continues to brew a regular selection of beer as well as some seasonal specialities. The main problem is capacity due to the small size of the brewhouse. One very recent development is the installation of bottling equipment, resulting in the launch of two new niche beers.

Availability
The beers are available on draught in the brewpub. Cask-conditioned versions are distributed into the UK

by Hilden Brewery and can also be found in Tara's Speciality Beerhouse in Killaloe/Ballina, County Tipperary. The bottles are currently being distributed to selected off-licenses in Ireland by Eurobeers, a Cork based distributor.

Visiting
The brewery is not open to the public but the mashing and brewing equipment can be seen from inside the pub.

Brewing at Messrs Maguires

The current brewer is Cuilan Loughnane who is very passionate about craft brewing, having developed an interest in brewing while working in Canada. When he moved back to Ireland, he heard that Dwan's brewpub was opening in Thurles, County Tipperary, and he got a job there. A few months later, the head brewer left and Cuilan took over the post. Unfortunately Dwan's closed, but Messrs Maguires were looking for a brewer at this time and Cuilan came to work in Dublin.

The brewery is on two levels. The mash tun and brew kettle are located on the ground floor and are visible from the bar. Fermentation and conditioning goes on in the cellar underneath the pub. The output is around fifteen hectolitres per brew and output for a year is usually about six hundred hectolitres. Rusty, the red ale, and Weiss dominate the output.

The Dublin mains water is very soft and excellent for lager brewing. For other beers, some treatment is necessary.

Cuilan only brews once a week due to capacity constraints. As he still lives in Tipperary, another member of staff starts the mash at 7 am. Their stouts and ales mash at between 66-67°C, while the lagers and wheat beers mash at the slightly lower temperature of 63-64°C. Mashing usually lasts ninety minutes. The kit is set up for pellet hops and these are added to the wort in the brew kettle during the ninety-minute boil.

The hopped wort is then cooled before fermentation. Most fermentations are done in the two closed conical fermenters whilst the sole open fermenter is used for the stouts and Weiss. Ales and stouts are fermented with an Irish ale yeast that is ordered from Oregon and, within forty-eight hours of being ordered, it finds itself pitched into the hopped wort. They are fermented for four days at around 20°C and then cool for two days, down to 3°C, prior to conditioning. Lagers are fermented at a lower temperature, 12°C, for a week, using a Bavarian lager yeast, before being cooled to 0°C over three days. A Bavarian wheat beer yeast ferments the Weiss for two days at 18°C. After a day cooling to 0°C, it is ready to be kegged in an unfiltered state where it will condition still further. Cuilan tends to brew one big batch of Weiss, enough for around

three months, he then ditches the yeast, using a fresh supply for the next brew.

The beers, with the exception of the Weiss, are then conditioned at around 2°C, with the ales and stouts getting two weeks. Lagers get anything from three to five weeks, depending on demand. As Cuilan only has three conditioning tanks at his disposal, sometimes the lagers simply have to be kegged earlier than he would like in order to to free up space for the next batch of green beer. The beers are then filtered en route to the bright beer tank and kegged, apart from the cask-conditioned and bottle-conditioned beers, which will take some yeast with them from the conditioning tanks.

Two draught beers are brewed all year round – Weiss and Rusty – with another three changing during the year. One of the changing beers will always be a stout or porter. Another will either be Haus – a German malty style lager – or Pils – a pilsner style lager. The third beer is also a lager, recent brews have been a Munich lager for the autumn and a bock, or strong, lager for Christmas.

WEISS

South German-style wheat beer
Alcohol: 5.1%

Messrs' Weiss has a grist of half Munich malt and half wheat malt. Hopping is very low, and only at the start of the boil. Weiss is a hazy pale-gold colour with a fruity, bubblegum nose alongside the dominant clove aroma. It is lively, firm and tart in the mouth, with a fruity tang. The finish has a nice acidity, with an almost grapefruit-like tartness developing into a fruity sweetness. This is a good interpretation of the style: less sweet than other Irish interpretations, with more spiciness and tartness to the fore.

RUSTY

Irish red ale
Alcohol: 4.6%

Rusty is mainly made with pale malt but with some Munich malt for sweetness and flaked barley for mouthfeel. A touch of wheat malt is also added to aid head retention. The yeast strain and the use of US hops makes this a very fruity interpretation of the style. A large proportion of nitrogen on dispense makes for a creamy head, while the body is deep bronze to tawny in colour. The nose and palate are fruity, nutty and malty, with a citric dryness in the finish, and lingering hop bitterness. Rusty is a flavoursome and enjoyable red ale, and not as sweet as many of the style. Rusty should stand up well to roasted-meat dishes.

BOCK

German-style bock (strong) lager
Alcohol: 6.5%

The Bock is one of two bottle-conditioned products. The grist mainly uses lager malt, but with a good proportion of Munich malt for sweetness, flavour and colour. The hops are predominantly Hersbrucker and other typical German hop varieties. The beer is copper in colour and has a haylike, malty bouquet, with a possible citrus edge. In the mouth it is full-bodied and rich, syrupy and malty, and the finish is warming, hoppy and long-lasting. The richness of the flavours makes it feel stronger than its 6.5 percent. This is an excellent and complex beer, and its richness would match roasted meats and ribs.

PORTER

Alcohol: 5.0%

Dublin is known for its stout but has, along the way, almost forgotten that porter was part of that history. Cuilan aims to put that right with his bottle-conditioned Porter. Pale malt is joined by black malt, for coffee-chocolate flavours, and amber malt, to get dryness but without the strong roastiness of a dry stout. Brewed as a porter and less bitter than a stout, only Northdown hops are used at the start of the boil. No aroma hops are added so the flavours of the malts can shine through. Porter is deep tawny in colour but not totally opaque. It has a luxurious dark-chocolate-and-cream aroma and flavour. The finish has an espresso-like dryness, with a lingering dark-chocolate bitterness making this a most fulsome and fully flavoured beer, to match sweet, chocolatey desserts.

THE PORTERHOUSE BREWING COMPANY

16-18 Parliament Street, Dublin 2
T: +353 (0)1 671 5715
W:www.porterhousebrewco.com
E:info@porterhousebrewco.com

The Porterhouse is one of the major success stories of the first wave of new Irish breweries. Established in 1996 by Oliver Hughes and Liam LaHarte as a brewpub in the Temple Bar district of Dublin, it has now grown into a separate brewery servicing five pubs.

Oliver had spent some time in England where he developed a love for beer, especially cask-conditioned ale. He also brewed over in England and then back home at the ill-fated Dempsey's ale brewery in Dublin. He first worked together with Liam LaHarte at Harty's in Blessington, another shortlived venture. However, in the late '80s, Oliver and Liam opened the first Porterhouse pub in Bray, selling a wide range of imported bottled beers. This was an experiment to see if the drinking public would take to different beers.

The experiment worked and the Porterhouse Temple Bar was the next step. The large range of imported beers remained but they went a step further to insulate themselves from the mass-marketed global brands by brewing their own draught beers. To do this they installed a brewery in the pub. They opened in a blaze of publicity, calling one of their lagers 'Weiser buddy'. Anheuser-Busch, the owners of Budweiser, were not pleased to say the least, and the Porterhouse was threatened with injunctions claiming that they were passing off their beer as Budweiser. Far from it, they argued, as the Porterhouse beer was unpasteurised and chemical-free so that you would be a wiser buddy to drink it! The next brush with the legal system was over another lager called 'Probably', which had a label that looked rather similar to a large Danish brand. Both of these products changed their name in due course, but these stunts gained the Porterhouse some great publicity. Brewing continued in Temple Bar until capacity constraints forced a change. A new purpose-built brewery began operating in 2000 on a business park in Ballycoolin on the outskirts of Dublin. Brewing continued in Temple Bar until 2001, when they reluctantly decided to concentrate production at the Ballycoolin site. Porterhouse like to argue that theirs is the largest genuine Irish brewery as the other bigger breweries are all part of global corporations based outside Ireland.

A third Porterhouse opened in London's Covent Garden in 2000, joined more recently by two back home: one in Glasnevin and one on Nassau Street in the heart of Dublin. The future looks bright indeed and they are planning to expand to other locations in Ireland, bringing their excellent beers to new audiences.

Availability
Porterhouse beers are available on draught at the Porterhouse pubs whilst Temple Bräu is available at other locations in the Temple Bar district of Dublin. And if you see Oyster Stout in northern Italy, it does indeed hail from the Porterhouse!

Visiting
The brewery is not open to the public.

Brewing the Porterhouse Range
There are ten beers in the regular range and the current head brewer is Peter Mosley, originally from Yorkshire. He has a Masters in brewing and distilling from Heriot-Watt University near Edinburgh and has worked at a number of English breweries as a brewer and head brewer.

All the brewing equipment is fairly new and purpose-built for the Ballycoolin brewhouse, which can brew 65 hectolitres a batch and turns out around 9,000 hectolitres in a year, with the lagers accounting for about half of this. They do not always brew a full batch as the philosophy is to have their beer as fresh as possible. This means that they do some half brews for products with lesser demand. Brewing usually takes place between three and four times a week.

The pale malt comes from Minch Norton and mains water provides the brewing liquor. Untreated, the liquor is hard, which is fine for the ales and stouts whilst it is softened for the lagers.

The mash lasts an hour for the lagers and Weiss, while the ales get an extra thirty minutes. The temperature varies depending on the product but is between 64 and 67°C. In the brew kettle the picture is reversed as the stouts and ales get an hour, with the lager and Weiss getting ninety minutes. Pellet hops are used with Galena and Nugget as the kettle hops for each beer.

The hopped wort is cooled by passing it through a heat exchanger, bringing the temperature down to 12°C for the lagers and 18°C for the other beers. The Weiss ferments for four days using a standard wheat beer yeast and is kept at around 19-20°C. The ales also ferment for four days but have a two-strain yeast that is specific to the Porterhouse. The temperature is held at 21°C to prevent the yeast from developing too many fruity flavours in the final beer. The lagers are fermented using a standard lager yeast for five days at 14°C.

After a three-day cooling period in the fermentation vessels, the beers make their way to the conditioning tanks. Ales and stouts spend four days here at 3°C. The stouts are kegged after adjusting the carbonation and, as the brewery has its own nitrogenator, are nitrogenated on site. Unlike the stouts, the ales are filtered after conditioning and the carbonation adjusted before kegging and the Porterhouse Red is nitrogenated. TSB is a cask-conditioned ale and is treated somewhat differently. TSB is not filtered and goes straight into the cask and will therefore have some yeast creating a natural sparkle as it matures, or conditions in cask. Isinglass finings are added to bring the yeast out of suspension and collect it at the bottom of the cask, giving a bright final product in the glass.

The lagers condition for two weeks at just over 1°C though Hersbrucker gets three times that, producing an excellent mellow pilsner style lager. The lagers are then filtered and the carbonation increased, as not enough will be generated during conditioning. The Weiss conditions for four to five days to increase its clarity. It is not filtered so the final product has the hazy quality expected of the hefe-weiss style.

One thing that marks the Porterhouse out is the large quantity of malt and hops used, more than most brewers, giving their beers a full-flavoured quality. They also make a point of not using any chemicals. Some of their ten regular beers are aimed to fit in with current Irish drinking habits, being closely modelled on popular beers, whilst others target those in search of a somewhat different, distinctive beer. As well as the ten regular beers, they also brew a changing range of one-off or seasonal beers, often to coincide with one of their beer festivals.

CHILLER

North American-style lager
Alcohol: 4.2%

This is the beer formerly known as 'Weiser buddy'. Chiller aims to be broadly similar to the popular standard lagers of North America, with the polar bear on the label suggesting that the beer will be wet and cold.

The grist is exclusively lager malt with a dash of rice to get a very pale final product. The beer is very lightly hopped both for bitterness and aroma, with the late hops being Cascade and US Fuggles.

Chiller is a very pale straw colour and has a light, delicate, slightly malty nose. The light hopping makes for a very gentle bitterness on the palate. There is a hint of tartness in the short, delicately bitter finish. Chiller is a light, clean and fairly simple refreshing lager.

TEMPLE BRÄU

European-style lager
Alcohol: 4.3%

Originally released under the litigation-attracting name of 'Probably', Temple Bräu is in the style of mainstream European lagers.

Lager malt makes up around 95 percent of the grist, with caramalt providing the balance, for a deeper colour than Chiller and a bit more malt character. Hallertau, Perle and Hersbrucker hops are added at the boil end for a subtle aromatic hop character.

Temple Bräu is slightly deeper in colour than Chiller, but no more than pale gold in colour. There is some citrus fruit evident on the nose joined by delicate floral notes. On the palate there is a touch of spiciness and herbal qualities derived from the hops. The finish has a little light citric fruit and a good level of hop bitterness that dries the mouth, all making for a more robust lager than Chiller.

HERSBRUCKER

Czech Pilsner-style lager
Alcohol: 5.0%

Hersbrucker is named after the aroma hop used at the end of the boil. Substantial quantities of it are used to make a lager with a distinctive noble hop aroma. Good quantities of Nugget and Galena are also used to give the lager a high level of hop bitterness reminiscent of Czech pilsners.

Hersbrucker pours a full gold colour with a classic floral and grassy pilsner nose. Smooth on the palate with some spicy hops at play. There is a long-lasting robust hop bitterness in the finish, leaving the drinker wanting more. Hersbrucker is easily the most characterful of the Porterhouse lagers and has a great finish. The high hopping and six weeks lagering make for superb pilsner-style lager, which would be a good accompaniment for chicken dishes as well as fish, especially if fried in batter.

HAUS WEISS

South German-style unfiltered wheat beer
Alcohol: 5%

The grist for Haus Weiss is made up with half wheat malt and half pale malt. As expected with this style of beer, hopping is low with a little Perle and Spalt added for aroma.

Pale gold in colour and slightly hazy, the dominant aromas are banana and bubblegum due to the wheat beer yeast that is used. Vanilla is also present on the nose, though on the palate is exhibited more as butterscotch, caramel or toffee. The bananas remain on the palate and into the gentle finish. Unlike many wheat beers of this style, Haus Weiss only exhibits a hint of tartness in the finish and does not have a pronounced yeasty bite. Nevertheless, it is a very flavoursome and refreshing wheat beer packed with banana fruitiness that would be a particularly good accompaniment for fruity desserts.

PORTERHOUSE RED

Irish red ale
Alcohol: 4.4%

An Irish red ale with a far more complicated grist than most. Pale malt makes up around 85 percent but is joined by crystal, chocolate and black malts for colour and flavour and some wheat flour to aid head retention. East Kent Goldings are added at the end of the boil to give the beer a fruity ale character.

Mahogany-red in colour with a creamy white head due to nitrogenation. The nose is malty with a light fruitiness. The nitrogenation makes for a smooth palate, lightly fruity with a shortish, slightly bitter finish. Porterhouse Red is an easy-drinking red ale with a good maltiness, balanced by hop bitterness in the finish.

TSB

English-style bitter
Alcohol: 3.7%

TSB is short for Turner's Sticklebract Bitter and it is based on the English concept of a session bitter – a beer lower in alcohol and easy drinking. TSB was created to celebrate the opening of Porterhouse Covent Garden which was built on the location of Turner's birthplace, hence the name. Brewed as an English bitter but with a twist – the addition of the New Zealand Sticklebract hop for aroma and flavour.

Crystal and roast malt together with roasted barley make up around 10 percent of the grist with the balance being pale malt. TSB used to be late hopped exclusively with Sticklebract but now also has some Styrian Goldings for fruitiness. The aroma hops are added twice, ten minutes before boil end and again at the end.

TSB pours a bright copper colour and has a biscuity malt nose with some pineapple fruitiness. The palate is slightly citric, which goes on to dry the mouth with the good hop bitterness, all hallmarks of this style. TSB is a very enjoyable session bitter with a fullness of flavour expected of a cask-conditioned ale.

AN BRAIN BLÁSTA

Strong ale
Alcohol: 7.0%

Brain Blásta is loosely translated from the Irish language as 'the tasty drop' and, of course, also has connotations in English for a strong ale. Pale malt only makes up 70 percent of the grist here leaving space for good quantities of roast malt, chocolate malt and caramalt for colour and to add significant malty and fruity flavours. Some wheat malt is also added to aid head retention.

The ale is hopped ten minutes before the end of the boil and again at boil end with Liberty from the US, East Kent Goldings and Fuggles. To get a strong hop nose to balance the malt and alcohol, a hop tea is made from English Fuggles and added to the fermenting vessel, contributing to a good hop bitterness in the final beer. Brain Blásta is dispensed by mixed gas rather than nitrogenated to retain more of its character.

Brain Blásta is deep copper, almost tawny in colour, with a rich, fruity nose featuring a pronounced dark-fruit aroma hinting at blackcurrants. The palate is rich and chewy with a fruitcake flavour. The alcohol provides a warming finish with peppery hops balancing the fruitiness and a distinct bitter orange note. A very complex and rich ale, one for those seeking a fully-flavoured ale but, as they say down the Porterhouse, 'use it, don't abuse it'.

PLAIN PORTER

Alcohol: 4.3%

Made to appeal to drinkers of Dublin's other famous stout, Plain Porter has a greater roasty character and fuller flavour. Pale malt makes up roughly 80 percent of the grist joined by crystal malt, with roast malt and roasted barley adding the signature roastiness, colour and body. There is also a little flaked barley for body. The aroma and flavour hop used is East Kent Goldings to add a touch of fruitiness to the final beer.

Plain has a creamy, off-white head and a black body with orange-red highlights. There is a lovely, enticing aroma of vanilla and milk chocolate against a background of roasted grains. The chocolate possibly turns dark on the palate which retains a good roastiness and creaminess while keeping the good porter characteristics of light body and restrained bitterness. The finish is also restrained in its bitterness and tanginess, whilst the roasty element continues unabated. A full flavoured porter with some stout characteristics but retains good porter qualities by not being too hoppy in the finish. A more roasty rather than fruity interpretation of porter.

OYSTER STOUT

Alcohol: 4.8%

Oysters and stout are said to be a classic food combination so here is a stout with oysters already added. The mash is pale malt, roasted malt, roasted barley and flaked barley. East Kent Goldings are added at the end of the boil with fresh oysters.

Oyster Stout has a black body with red highlights and a creamy coloured head. It is roasty on the nose with a discernible whiff of fish and iodine. Sweeter than the other stouts on the palate with that fishy quality again. The finish is low in bitterness and somewhat short. Oyster Stout is possibly an acquired taste but interesting nonetheless.

WRASSLERS XXXX STOUT

Irish dry stout
Alcohol: 5.0%

Reputedly made to a recipe originally brewed at Deasy's Brewery, Clonakilty in west Cork, which was a favourite of Michael Collins. It certainly aims to be a full-flavoured old-style stout. The complex grist contains pale malt, roasted malt, roasted barley, flaked barley and wheat malt. East Kent Goldings are the flavouring hop added ten minutes before the end of the boil and again at the end. The uncompromising bitterness is assisted by adding a hop tea during fermentation.

Wrasslers has a dark creamy, almost beige head with a jet black body. There is a strong roasted aroma joined by bitter chocolate and coffee. The palate is reminiscent of black coffee with a strong roastiness and is almost charcoal-like. Wrasslers has a very long assertive bitter finish, dry and hoppy. This is a stout that certainly packs a punch and is not for the faint hearted. It is uncompromisingly dry and fully flavoured with an intense more-ish bitterness, without doubt one of the very best Irish stouts. So robust is Wrasslers that it could stand up well to smoked fish dishes as well as chocolate-rich desserts.

SMITHWICK'S

**St Francis Abbey Brewery,
Parliament Street, Kildare**
T: +353 (0)56 772 1014
W: www.diageo.com

On the banks of the River Nore in the heart of Kilkenny lies the remains of the twelfth-century St Francis Abbey. It stands as a reminder of brewing's monastic past in the yard of the brewery that now bears its name

It is claimed that this is Ireland's oldest operating brewery, dating back to 1710. However, the claim is hard to substantiate. John Smithwick and a Richard Cole did obtain a lease for a small property near the abbey from the estate of the Duke of Ormonde around this time, but there is no mention of brewing in the document.

Most brewers at this time were either brewhouses for the gentry, small farmhouse operations, or alehouses brewing and selling beer on the premises for immediate consumption. Whether Messrs Smithwick and Cole were running an alehouse is not known. Whatever the truth, John Smithwick and his family made a great deal of money in land and commercial dealings – especially in trading tea, a scarce commodity at the time.

The first definite brewing Smithwick was Edmund Smithwick. Edmund bought a brewery and distillery at St Francis Abbey from the Second Duke of Ormonde in 1827 and was very successful. Edmund was a noted philanthropist and collaborated with his rivals Sullivan's Brewery in setting up a soup kitchen in 1847 during the Great Famine. By the 1850s, he was brewing seven beers – Extra Stout, Porter, X Ale, XX Ale, Pale Ale Butt, Harvest Beer and East India Pale Ale – for sale locally and for export. Output had gone up from 5,000 barrels in 1850 to 40,000 ten years later, making Smithwick's the largest brewer in Ireland outside of Dublin and Cork. However, this was not to last, and a period of decline set in, mainly due to the loss of trade in England, as British brewers began building up estates of tied houses. By 1900, output had fallen below 10,000 barrels as Smithwick's concentrated on the Kilkenny area.

James Smithwick took over in 1900, and the brewery was producing five different beers – Extra Stout, Porter, Pale Ale Butt, Premium Pale Ale and Dinner Ale. By 1910, trade had recovered, mainly due to the fact that the company obtained the contract to supply the British army barracks in Belfast. By the eve of the First World War, Smithwick's output had risen to 15,000 barrels. In the same year, 1914, they took over and closed their Kilkenny rivals Sullivan's Brewery on James Street.

In 1921, a long strike paralysed the company. Guinness moved in to supply stout and porter, thus taking Smithwick's trade: the brewery would never brew stout and porter again. They now had two brands, Pale Ale and Premium Pale Ale.

The 1930s were a good decade for Smithwick's, as their new brand – No. 1 Ale, which replaced Pale Ale Butt – achieved great success, and overall production at the brewery reached 20,000 barrels. Buoyed by this, they developed No. 1 Ale into a national brand, which was also a success. At this time, they were also brewing Harvest Festival Beer and Pale Ale XX. This range was extended in 1948 with the development of a sweet winter ale called Smithwick's Barley Wine.

By 1950, output was approaching 52,000 barrels, and the only competition they had in the Irish ale market was smaller brewers selling beer in their own regional catchment areas. In 1953, they expanded by buying the Great Northern Brewery in Dundalk. This was soon to be superfluous, however, due to the modernisation of the Kilkenny plant following a bacteriological infection. In 1954, a strain of lactic-acid bacteria got into the plant. The loss of trade due to this infection resulted in the decision being taken to change to a sterile plant. Out went wooden barrels and cask-conditioned beer and in came metal kegs and chill-filtration technology. The modern plant was able to meet the needs of the company, so the Great Northern Brewery was leased to a Guinness-led consortium in 1957 and then sold

outright to them three years later.

In 1961, Irish Ale Breweries was created when the Guinness owned Cherry-Cairnes Group merged with Dundalk's Macardle Moore, owned by the British-based Allied Breweries. By joining together as Irish Ale Breweries, they immediately had a national distribution for their Phoenix and Double Diamond brands, from Waterford and Dundalk respectively. To combat this new enemy, Smithwick's No. 1 Ale and Barley Wine were rebranded 'Time'. They initially performed well, with output at the brewery hitting an all-time high of 74,000 barrels. However, the company was not able to sustain this boom, and sales began to fall in the face of the competition from both Irish Ale Breweries and the British Watney's Red Barrel, brewed by Murphy's of Cork. By mid-decade, output was down to 56,000 barrels, and the moniker 'Time' was discontinued and the family name used again.

This downturn led to the momentous decision to join Irish Ale Breweries rather than try to compete against them. This was the beginning of the end of family involvement in the brewery. Walter Smithwick retired in 1965, to be replaced by Peter, who would be the last Smithwick to be involved in the company. The year 1965 was also a significant one for the development of draught Smithwick's. No. 1 Ale was a pale ale, but the Irish market seemed to avour a sweeter and less bitter product, and so No. 1 Ale was reformulated for sale as Smithwick's Draught.

This new Smithwick's Ale sold 15,000 barrels in 1966. Ales were popular with the younger generation, who were slowly moving away from stout. Smithwick's had little competition in this market, so sales quickly soared, reaching 495,000 barrels in 1979. However, it was soon to be replaced by the newest phenomenon: lager. Significant investment took place in 1980, and although output hit 600,000 barrels in 1981, demand would soon begin to fail off.

In 1986, the brewery won the contract to brew Budweiser for the Irish market. Two years later, Irish Ale Breweries was dissolved and the brewery, along with others in the former company, became fully owned by Guinness Ireland. Peter Smithwick left at this time, meaning that the Smithwick family were no longer involved in the brewery. The brewing of Smithwick's Barley Wine was transferred to Dundalk and has now stopped completely. At one time, the brewery even stopped brewing Smithwick's Ale as production was transferred to Waterford. Smithwick's is now back at its home in Kilkenny and is also brewed at the Great Northern Brewery in Dundalk. Smithwick's, however, makes up only around 5 percent of the output at Kilkenny, with Budweiser dominating the remainder. Kilkenny Ale, a nitrogenated beer, is also brewed there.

Availability

Smithwick's is available throughout Ireland and in the US. Kilkenny Ale has a smaller availability in Ireland. Its top markets are Canada and Australia, but it is available elsewhere in Europe and in some Far Eastern countries.

Visiting

It is possible to visit the brewery during the months of June, July and August. Visits take place at 3 pm Monday to Friday, and tickets can be collected at security. Visitors are taken to the Cellar Bar, where they watch an audiovisual presentation and later have an opportunity to taste the beer.

Brewing at St Francis Abbey

Unfortunately Diageo were unable to provide up-to-date information regarding brewing at St Francis Abbey Brewery. Therefore this description of brewing may not be entirely reflective of current practice.

The grist for Smithwick's Ale is mainly pale malt, with a dash of roasted barley for colour. Mashing lasts one hour, at around 67°C. The wort is clarified in a lauter tun before going to the brew kettle. The boil lasts ninety minutes, and there are three hop additions. Northdown and

Target are added at the start of the boil as bittering hops are joined by Challenger a little way into the boil. Goldings is the aroma hop and is added towards the end of the boil. Glucose is added during the boil for that signature Smithwick's sweetness.

The hopped wort is fermented for four days in huge closed-conical fermenters using what is probably a descendant of the original Smithwick's yeast. The green beer is then chilled to crop the yeast, and conditions for five to seven days at 0°C. The beer is then chill-filtered to remove any remaining residue before being sent to the bright beer tank, where the carbonation is adjusted. It is then ready to be kegged or packaged in bottle or can.

As well as brewing Budweiser under licence and Kilkenny Ale, the plant kegs Cashel's Cider, which is made in England for Diageo.

SMITHWICK'S

Irish red ale
Alcohol: 3.8%

The brewery's flagship beer, and Ireland's most popular ale. Smithwick's is reddish-amber in colour, with malty, fruity and toffeeish notes. It is malty on the palate, with a slight sweetness. The finish is delicately bitter and about right for the style. Smithwick's is not the most fully-flavoured of the Irish red ales on the market but is a refreshing if somewhat untaxing beer.

KILKENNY

Irish red ale
Alcohol: 4.3%

Kilkenny was launched in the late 1980s as the nitrogenated counterpart to Smithwick's. It is currently brewed in both Kilkenny and Dublin. It is a deep reddish-amber beer, with a nice fruitiness akin to pear drops, toffee notes and some biscuity malt. In the mouth it is fairly light in body and, thanks to the nitrogenation, smooth, while being quite fully flavoured, with malt and fruit to the fore. There is a suggestion of dark fruit on the finish, which has a nice bitterness and is mouth-drying. Kilkenny is a decent ale and has a touch more hop bitterness than many interpretations of the style.

STRANGFORD LOUGH BREWING COMPANY

Braidleigh Lodge, 22 Shore Road, Killyleagh, County Down
T: +44 (0)28 4482 1461
W: www.slbc.ie
E: contact@slbc.ie

The Strangford Lough Brewing Company is named after the beautiful marine lough in County Down and started life in 2004 when two businessmen, Bob Little and Tony Davies, were looking at possible merchandising for the St Patrick's Centre in Downpatrick. Beer was not an initial interest but they learnt that the US trademark for 'St Patrick's Ale' and its derivatives were lapsing so they decided to acquire it. They subsequently found that no one owned the trademark for the EU so they acquired that one as well.

The next step was to brew beers to utilise the trademarks. However, as businessmen rather than brewers, they realised that building a brewery was not necessary in order to launch a new range of beers. They also knew that building a brewery would be capital-intensive and that small breweries without outlets often find it tough going. The practices of bigger brewers provided the inspiration for the model they adopted. Big multi-national brewers tend not to build new breweries when launching their product in a new country but instead license an existing brewery to brew their beer. Therefore, they decided to license other brewers to make their beer to see if a market could be created before possibly establishing a brewery at a later date.

Brewers were approached to devise a number of recipes, which were subsequently narrowed down by market testing. These beers were branded with local themes and the challenge was then to get them out to the marketplace. The beers have proved popular and enjoy a wide distribution in Northern Ireland, the US and beyond. Building a brewery in or around Killyleagh remains a medium-term objective.

The beers are currently brewed in England and brewing also takes place in the US for the North American market. Each bottle is emblazoned with a droplet symbolising a drop of water from Strangford Lough. The beers are all bottle-conditioned, as it was decided that a niche beer would appeal to a certain market and not compete with big brands. Also, in the US craft beer is huge, and it was thought that a bottle-conditioned beer would appeal to those interested in craft brewing.

They have been successful to date and their beers are selling well. They currently sell five products, three in the St Patrick's range and two in the Viking range. The St Patrick's range have some shamrock added to the brew in liquefied form. The future of one of the St Patrick's range – St Patrick's Gold – is currently under consideration and has not been reviewed here.

ST PATRICK'S BEST

English-style bitter
Alcohol: 3.8%

This is a session bitter of moderate strength. The image on the label is of Saul Church, the first church St Patrick founded in Ireland. The malts are pale, crystal and black and the wort is hopped with Challenger and First Gold for bitterness, with a late addition of Goldings for aroma and flavour. The beer pours a copper colour and has a nutty, sweet-scented, fruity aroma. Bitter hops in the mouth and on the somewhat mouth-drying finish, which has a hint of fruitiness. This is a good-quality everyday-drinking beer.

ST PATRICK'S ALE

Strong ale
Alcohol: 6.0%

This strong ale features the statue of St Patrick above the village of Raholp in County Down, where he is said to

have died. Pale malt is joined by crystal and black malts in the grist and the hopping is a blend of Goldings, Progress and Challenger. Dark tawny in colour, it has a malty, treacle-toffee nose and a rich, roasty and malty palate. The finish is rich and long-lasting, with a roasty dryness.

St Patrick's Ale is an excellent, full-flavoured, rich and warming strong ale that could be an excellent accompaniment to beef or lamb dishes and possibly some game

BARELEGS BREW

Golden ale
Alcohol: 4.5%

Magnus Barelegs was a Viking and King of Norway from 1093 to 1103. He regularly raided Britain and Ireland, however, his raid on Downpatrick in 1103 was to be his last as he was killed by the local warriors. The grist is pale ale and lager malt with some caramalt and flaked maize for additional flavour. The bittering hops is Northern Brewer; the late hops are First Gold and Perle.

This beer in golden in colour and

had a fruity nose dominated by pears with a hint of vanilla in the background. The palate is also fruity and bitter-sweet and the finish exhibits a subtle bitterness. Barelegs is refreshing and delicious, working well as an appetiser or possibly as a match for some soft cheeses.

LEGBITER

Golden ale
Alcohol: 4.8%

Legbiter was the name given to Magnus Barelegs' sword and it is still on display today in Oslo. Legbiter has a similar grist to Barelegs but without the pale ale malt and therefore has lager malt, caramalt and flaked maize. Bittering hops are a blend of Northern Brewer and First Gold, Goldings and Styrian Goldings are the aroma hops.

Like Barelegs Brew, Legbiter is golden in colour but there is a difference in the bouquet. Here there are mown hay and spicy notes with some fruitiness, but this time oranges are the dominant fruit aroma. More fruit and spice in the mouth and the finish is delicately bitter and has a fruity hint. Another enjoyable and refreshing golden ale.

WHITEWATER BREWING COMPANY

**40 Tullyframe Road,
Kilkeel, County Down**
T: +44 (0)28 4176 9449
W: www.whitewaterbrewing.co.uk
E: info@whitewaterbrewing.co.uk

The Whitewater Brewery is set in the stunningly beautiful landscape of rural south County Down. It nestles on the south eastern slopes of the majestic mountains of Mourne, near the village of Kilkeel. The brewery is named after the White Water River that starts high up in the Mourne Mountains and flows past the brewery.

The owner and head brewer is Bernard Sloan and the brewery stands on what is still the Sloan family farm. Bernard worked in England for some time in the dairy industry before, by chance, becoming involved with a brewpub in Manchester. This fired his interest in brewing and he decided he wanted to start a craft brewery in Northern Ireland.

In 1996 the Whitewater Brewery was established on a very small scale in what was the old potato shed. The pub trade in Northern Ireland was then pretty much a closed market, split between the Guinness/Tennents-Bass duopoly, a problem that still persists to this day. However, Whitewater made steady growth and a new building was erected to house the expanding operation.

Bernard has nevertheless been very active in getting his cask-conditioned ales into pubs in Northern Ireland and now, having installed a state-of-the-art bottling line, has just started bottling. By moving into the bottled market he is able to get into more pubs and, importantly, off-licences.

Availability

Whitewater's cask-conditioned ale is available at a number of pubs in Belfast such as the Crown, McHugh's, Ryan's, Kings Head and the Kitchen Bar as well as others, the White Horse in Saintfield – which is also owned by Bernard – the Hillside in Hillsborough, Daft Eddy's in Killinchy and Gillespies in Bangor. The new bottled range is beginning to make its presence felt and is currently on offer at Sainsbury's stores across Northern Ireland, a number of off-licences in County Down, as well as several pubs in Belfast and will no doubt be much more widely available in the near future.

Brewing at Whitewater

Since Inbev closed Thomas Caffrey's old Mountain Brewery in Belfast, Whitewater is now the largest brewery in Northern Ireland. The brewery has a brew length of around 20 hectolitres and typically brews twice a week, with a yearly output in excess of 1500 hectolitres – an output dominated by Belfast Ale.

The equipment has been assembled over the years from various sources and it and the brewery are kept scrupulously clean. The brewing liquor comes from the local mains supply, fed from a reservoir in the Mourne Mountains, but there is a well on site which may be used in the future. The liquor is burtonised but not heavily so. Pale malt is supplied by Minch Norton in Athy.

The brewing day starts at 7 am, with an infusion mash lasting ninety minutes at around 65 to 67°C, the darker the brew the higher the temperature tends to be. The darkness of the brew also affects the boil which lasts in the region of sixty to ninety minutes, with darker brews pushing towards the ninety minute mark. The kettle is set up for pellet hops and Bernard uses quite a bit of US hops in his beers.

A heat exchanger cools the hopped wort down to 19°C for ales and lower for lager. Fermentation happens in closed conicals, employing two different yeasts. A single-strain lager yeast ferments at around 15°C, while the bi-strain ale yeast ferments in the low 20s to avoid generating too many esters, as the yeast can impart very fruity characteristics if allowed a free reign. The ale yeast is the one used since 1996 but its history goes back further. Both yeasts originate from the old Caffrey's Mountain Brewery in Belfast. Bernard used to do some engineering work up there and was given some of the culture which is still used today, providing a tangible link with Northern Ireland's brewing history.

The green beer is then cooled and racked into conditioning tanks. Beer destined to become cask-conditioned ale is conditioned at no more than 5°C for about two weeks before being put into cask, though the last casks from a particular tank may have had three weeks brewery conditioning. No yeast is added to the casks; they will take some residual yeast with them from the conditioning tanks and isinglass finings will be added to clarify the ale. The lager and bottled beers are conditioned at 0°C with the lager getting a minimum of three weeks lagering time in the conditioning tank, though a month's lagering is preferred. By the time the tank is emptied, some of the lager will have had six weeks lagering. The lager and bottled beers are then filtered and sent to the bright beer tank to adjust carbonation prior to bottling or kegging.

Whitewater brews four products year round but these are supplemented by a plethora of other cask-conditioned ales throughout the year, some seasonal, some not. Snake Drive appears for St Patrick's Day, Mayflower in May, Solstice Pale Ale and Bees Endeavour – a beer made with honey – during the summer, Nutbrown Ale for the autumn and Sanity Clause at Christmas time. Other ales are brewed once or twice a year at no fixed time and these include All that Jazz, Cascade, Dappled Mare, Mill Ale, Northern Brewer and White Gold, whilst the excellent Glen Ale is brewed around three times a year. Currently, two products are bottled but this is likely to increase as the lager is soon to be bottled. Also, a stout and pale ale are likely to be specifically developed for bottling.

BELFAST ALE

Irish ale
Alcohol: 4.5%

This is the brewery's flagship cask-conditioned beer, available all year round. It is also available in bottle. Slightly less hopped than an English bitter, so it is a bit of a hybrid, not quite an Irish red ale and not quite a bitter. Pale malt is joined by crystal and chocolate malts in the grist, with some malted wheat to aid head retention in the finished beer. Northdown, Challenger and Goldings are the bittering hops whilst Fuggles is used for late hopping.

Belfast ale is a dark amber colour with a malty and fruity – possibly strawberry-like – nose. Malty, nutty and earthy on the palate, the finish is drying but with a delicate bitterness. This is a lovely ale with excellent complexity of flavour bringing about a more-ish drink.

BLONDE

Pilsner-style lager
Alcohol: 4.0%

One of the newer brews created primarily for the White Horse Inn in Saintfield but soon to reach a wider audience in the bottle. The grist is all lager malt save for a bit of wheat flour to aid head retention. It is hopped with Challenger and Northdown at the start of the boil with the classic Saaz hop at boil end for that noble pilsner aroma.

A pale-straw-coloured beer, Blonde has a floral nose, courtesy of the Saaz, with a hint of citrus fruit. The palate is bitter-sweet with a certain tang before a clean, drying finish with good bitterness, exactly what would be expected from a good interpretation of the pilsner style. Blonde should pair well with fish and chicken dishes.

CROWN AND GLORY

Spiced ale
Alcohol: 3.8%

A cask-conditioned session beer, lower in strength than most beers and brewed for the Crown Bar in Belfast, though it can occasionally be found at the White Horse Inn, Saintfield. A small quantity of crystal malt joins the pale malt in the grist and the ale is hopped with Challenger and Northdown for bitterness and Fuggles for aroma. A small quantity of coriander is added to the brew kettle and, interestingly, more is added to the fermenter.

Crown and Glory pours a golden colour with a very fruity nose reminiscent of sweet orange marmalade. The coriander comes though a bit more on the complex palate, which is spicy, earthy and tangy. Some more spice is found on the finish, which starts with a light bitterness that increases its intensity as it develops in the mouth. This is a good, complex cask-conditioned ale but remains very easy-drinking.

CLOTWORTHY DOBBIN

Strong ale
Alcohol: 5.0%

Named after the owner of the predecessor brewery to Thomas Caffrey's in West Belfast, made to be enjoyed and savoured and available only in bottle. It has a complex grist, the chief ingredients of which are pale, crystal, chocolate and black malts. Challenger and Northdown are the bittering hops while the US Cascade hop is added at boil end for its fruity character.

It pours a dark red-brown and has a very rich and malty nose with dark fruits dominant and a hint of roasted grain. The palate is also malty with some spice, roasted grain and a possible suggestion of chocolate. The finish is long, with some malty sweetness in a beautiful balance with overtones of bitter chocolate. This is an excellent ale; very complex, fully flavoured, rich and fulsome – a great nightcap or winter warmer and a match for roasted red meats and rich food.

BREWERIES COMING SOON

The future is looking bright for craft brewing in Ireland, with the number of breweries set to increase in the near future. Interestingly, two of these forthcoming breweries plan to brew primarily for the local market in the same way that dozens of small Irish brewers did in the past.

Clifden, County Galway

This brewery is the brainchild of Barbara-Ann McCabe and Harry Joyce. Both have travelled and worked abroad but, on returning to Ireland, were disappointed with the lack of choice in pubs. They think the west of Ireland deserves a great local beer and are setting out to brew just that.

The brewery does not have a name yet but the plan is to brew a draught product for the local market. Clifden last had a brewery in the early 1800s and there has not been one in County Galway for a hundred years. This is all set to change as the brewhouse is virtually complete and should brew its first beer very soon.

Blue Stack Brewing Company
Ramelton, County Donegal
Tel: +353 (0) 749151012
Email: bluestack@mail.com

The majority shareholder and impetus behind Blue Stack Brewing is Edward McDaid. McDaid's are soft-drink manufacturers and wholesalers but used to bottle and condition Guinness. This is the inspiration, but this time they will do the brewing as well.

The company plans to use its own spring water and will brew a range of beers with local themes, starting with All Blacks Ale – the original captain of the New Zealand All Blacks rugby union team came from Ramelton – and Golden Eagle Lager – there are attempts to repopulate the nearby Glenveigh National Park with the Golden Eagle. This range will be increased with seasonal specialities.

Initially availability will be local and drinkers in north Donegal should be able to buy Blue Stack's beers from 2007. They will be available both as kegged draught beer and in bottles whilst cask-conditioned beer will be sold in Northern Ireland.

Shelta Brewery
Templemore,
County Tipperary

Plans for the Shelta Brewery are still at an early stage but the man behind them is Cuilan Loughnane, currently brewer for Messrs Maguire's in Dublin.

He plans to brew niche products mainly for export such as

traditionally brewed porters and stouts. They will have a relatively high alcoholic strength and be aged in oak vats for a number of months in the same way that old porter breweries used to do in their porter tun rooms.

Shelta hopes to be brewing in 2008.

Actons Pub
**Brook Lodge and Wells Spa,
Macreddin, County Wicklow
Telephone: +353 (0) 402 36444
Email: brooklodge@macreddin.ie
Website: www.brooklodge.com**

Acton's pub is situated in Macreddin Village, a resort in the heart of the Wicklow Mountains. It has a few brewing vessels and hopes to get more soon, together with an extension built to accommodate a craft brewery. The plan is to make beer with as few preservatives and chemicals as possible in keeping with the resort's philosophy.

Carysfort lager and Three Wells stout are currently available in Acton's Pub, but these are 'own label' versions of beer brewed by Messrs Maguires in Dublin.

A SHORT HISTORY OF CIDERMAKING IN IRELAND

Very little has been written about the history of cider in Ireland. However, what is known is that cider, like beer, is also an ancient drink with Celtic lineage. Cidermaking on a small scale took place in counties such as Armagh, Tipperary and Waterford. But, today, like brewing, cidermaking in Ireland is dominated by one big company, making it very difficult for smaller producers to enter the market.

The Early History of Cider

Sweet apples hail from Asia in the area around present-day Kazakhstan. Indeed the former Kazakh capital, Almaty, means 'father of apples'. They then spread east and west along the trade routes.

The small, harsh, acidic crab apple is a native species growing wild in Ireland and would have been used as a foodstuff by the native population, as it was in Britain. Records show that when Julius Cesar landed in England in 55BCE he came across native Britons drinking a form of cider. So taken was he with the drink that he began to enjoy it himself.

As well as a food source, apples would also have been used for making cider: a population that can brew beer can certainly make cider, as it is a much easier process.

Cidermaking is a very Celtic tradition and an early Welsh saint, St Teilo, took apples used for making cider to Normandy to establish an orchard there. However, it was the Normans invasion that would be the main catalyst for establishing cidermaking on a larger scale in Ireland.

Monks and Normans

Monasteries were not only early centres of brewing but, thanks to their orchards, were also sites of cidermaking. However, it would be the arrival of the Normans that would really establish the practice, as well as that of making perry from pears. With the Normans came new apple and pear varieties specifically bred for cider and perry-making and many orchards would have been planted during this time.

A key development in the thirteenth century was the invention of the screw press, allowing for the production of cider and perry on a larger scale.

The dissolution of the monasteries meant that production was transferred to the hands of the lay people and cidermaking became a farmhouse industry. Evidence suggests that there were many cider presses operating on farms in areas such as Tipperary and Armagh, with 'Blackwater' cider from County Waterford being particularly well known. Indeed, in certain parts of Ireland, for example, Tipperary and Limerick, it was known that cider was used to pay rent and the wages of farm labourers.

In Northern Ireland, County

The old days of repairing barrels at Bulmer's

Armagh is known as the Orchard County and has long been famous for its apples and cider. During the Williamite wars, King William stationed his cider-maker, Paul le Harper, there to supply his troops. By the middle of the nineteenth century, though, small-scale farmhouse cidermaking was in serious decline throughout Ireland.

William Magner

The major event that shaped Irish cidermaking started in 1935 when William Magner took over the closed Murphy Brewery in Clonmel and began making cider on a larger scale than had previously been seen. He quickly became successful and attracted the interest of the large English cidermaking company HP Bulmer of Herefordshire. They joined forces, before HP Bulmer eventually

took over the operation. Ownership has changed over the years, and the company is currently part of C&C Group plc. Magners, as Bulmers is known outside the Republic of Ireland, has become one of the success stories of recent times, with sales overseas showing unabated growth.

Small-scale farmhouse cidermaking pretty much died out around the same time. As farmers became more specialised, cidermaking became more of a distraction rather than an earner and the tradition of using it to pay farm labourers wages was outlawed. Also, the advent of an industrial-sized cider producer such as Bulmers/Magners made it easier for farmers to sell their apples to them for making cider rather than make it themselves, a bit like small brewers abandoning brewing and becoming bottlers for Guinness.

First steps towards craft cider

Unlike brewing, small-scale cidermaking in Ireland is in its infancy. The staggering growth of cider due to the Bulmers/Magners phenomenon is a double-edged sword. On the positive side they have revolutionised the image of cider and created a whole new group of cider drinkers. However, the negative side is that, such has been their success, people's image of cider is of a drink that is fizzy and sweet. Small-scale cidermaking is therefore somewhat hamstrung by the position Bulmers/Magners has in the market.

The other main problem for cidermakers in the Repubic of Ireland is that, unlike for the brewers, there is no duty rebate for cider. This means that small-scale farmhouse production is not encouraged. Nevertheless, some cider is made on a small scale and new producers are emerging in Armagh in a project that was initially funded by the Department for Agriculture and Rural Development. The cider is currently being sold as 'Mac's Cider', and the hope is that, by producing cider in the county, and using native apples, in the near future the name 'Armagh Cider' will become a protected geographical name, akin to the AC system for wine in France. They have the benefit of being in the United Kingdom, where farmhouse cidermaking is encouraged. Anyone making less than 70 hectolitres a year can sell their cider without it being subject to duty.

To really encourage small-scale craft cidermaking and bring the process back to its farmhouse origins, the Republic of Ireland should copy the UK example and allow small-scale cidermakers to sell without having to pay duty on what can be a quality farmhouse product. Furthermore, the quality and 'localness' of small-scale cidermaking should be emphasised by allowing small quantities to be sold at farmers' markets. The system in the UK has resulted in a growing number of excellent small-scale cider and perry producers making distinctive, characterful, local products that are very different from standardised mass-market industrial cider.

Interestingly, cidermaking remains popular in the Celtic fringe of Europe, with a large number of small-scale producers in Brittany as well as the Asturias and Basque regions of Spain. Also Welsh cider and perry are currently enjoying a major revival. It would be great if Ireland could develop more local small-scale ciders and join its Celtic cousins in making this most traditional of drinks.

Making Cider

Making cider is very different to brewing beer and is essentially like making wine. The basic ingredients are just apples and yeast. In the same way that grapes are crushed and the

sugars in the juice are fermented to produce wine, sugar-rich juice is extracted from apples and fermented to make cider.

The Apple Orchard

Cidermaking starts in the orchard. There are three basic types of apples. Dessert apples such as Cox's, culinary apples such as the Bramley, and cider apples. There is also the crab apple that grows wild in hedgerows, woodlands and in people's gardens, but it is not really cultivated on a large scale.

Cider can be made from any apples and Irish cider often contains a large quantity of the Irish Bramley. However, cider apples have certain advantages over the others as they have been cultivated over the years for the purpose of making cider. They produce good quantities of juice with a high sugar content and provide good tannins and apple taste to the final product.

In the same way that the grape variety will determine the final taste of wine, the apple variety chosen is significant for cider. However, unlike wine, most cider is a mixture of apples, though large-scale cider production involves many processes which make the actual selection of apple varieties of less consequence.

There are a huge number of cider apple varieties such as Breakwells Seedling, Tremletts Bitter, Dabinett, Yarlington Mill, Brown Snout and Kingston Black to name but a few. They are grouped depending on their acid and tannin: 'sweets' are low in both acid and tannin; 'bitter-sweets' low in acid but high in tannin; 'bittersharps', high in acid and tannin; and 'sharps' high in acid but low in tannin. The variety used by the cider-maker will depend on what they want to achieve in the final product.

Apples and pears ripen at different times, depending on their variety. Harvesting at the right time is crucial to avoid any off-flavours in the final cider and to ensure that the apple or pear has matured enough to provide a good quantity of sugar when pressed into juice. The main harvesting period stretches from late summer until around Christmas time. Traditionally apples and pears would have been handpicked but now harvesting is mechanised.

The Cider Mill

Cider is not brewed but rather made or produced and this happens in a cider mill. Production at the cider mill coincides with harvest time, producing a flurry of activity, whilst the rest of the year things are fairly quiet as the cider matures. The harvested apples will be delivered to the mill and roughly washed to remove stones and dirt. After this, the real process of cidermaking begins.

Milling and Pressing

To begin with, the apples are milled to a pulp. Roughly chopping the apples in this way aids juice extraction. The pulp is then pressed to extract the juice. The traditional way of pressing is to wrap a quantity of the pulp in a cloth – a process known as making a 'cheese'. A number of these cheeses are built up one on top of another with slatted racks in between. The cheeses are then pressed and the apple juice runs out whilst the solid leftovers, known as 'pomace', is held in the cloths. Pressing cider in this way is a batch process; you make a set of cheeses and extract the juice before having to construct another set of cheeses to get more juice.

Much cider is still made in this way but there are more modern continuous methods of juice extraction, such as conveying the pulp between rollers or high tension belts.

The apple juice will then often be treated to ensure a good fermentation. In a large-scale operation it will be analysed to check its sugar concentration and pH. If the sugar content is regarded as being too low to produce enough alcohol, the juice will be chaptelised, that is, sugar will be added. Food grade acid may also be added to get the pH right for a successful fermentation and avoid the development of off-flavours.

Wild yeasts grow on apple skins and will make their way into the juice. Some cidermakers will allow these to be involved in the fermentation but many will not as they can produce off-flavours in the final product. To suppress unwanted yeasts and bacteria, the juice will be treated with sulphur dioxide, a practice going back centuries that is also used in winemaking.

Fermentation

The juice will then be pumped into fermentation vats and be joined by yeast. Usually, a selected strain of yeast will be used for a consistent final product, as the result of using allowing wild yeasts to attack the juice can be unpredictable.

Fermentation will last anything from two to four weeks. Most cider-makers will ferment to dryness, that is, until the yeast has consumed all the sugar, creating alcohol, carbon dioxide and the many flavour compounds that will give character to the final product.

A cider fermented to dryness will be high in alcohol, around 7 percent or more and the yeast will begin to die and fall to the bottom. The 'raw cider', as it is now known, will be 'racked' off the spent yeast into maturation vats.

Maturation

Maturing the raw cider greatly improves its flavour. As the raw cider matures it becomes less harsh, more rounded, smooth and complex. Cider can be matured for anything from weeks to months and will be regularly tasted to decide when it is ready.

During maturation the cider may undergo a malo-lactic fermentation. Lactic acid bacteria converts the harsh malic acid from the apples into lactic acid which has around half the acidity, making the finished cider less sharp. The final cider will also be more complex as more flavour compounds are generated. Malo-lactic fermentation can happen spontaneously or be encouraged by using selected strains of bacteria. Depending on the style of cider desired, some cidermakers may choose to prevent malo-lactic fermentation from occurring.

Final Processing

Once fermentation is judged complete, the 'base cider' may undergo a number of further processes before reaching the glass, bottle or can.

Base ciders from the different vats will have different characteristics and may be blended together. The cider will then be 'made up' as required to achieve the desired final product. Making up can include adding sugar to make a medium or a sweet cider, adding potable water to bring the alcohol level down or the adding of colouring to give a consistent product. As there is no still cider currently for sale in Ireland, the cider will be carbonated.

The cider will then usually be filtered and possibly pasteurised before the 'finished cider' reaches the drinker in a clear state.

In the same way that some beers are bottle-conditioned, one cidermaker in Ireland bottle-conditions his cider. The cider will be bottled with some yeast, which then becomes a secondary fermentation. As it is enclosed, the carbon dioxide which is created will result in a natural sparkling cider.

Perry

Perry is made by a similar method from pears known as perry pears. There are a few different varieties, but there is very little perry pear orcharding in Ireland because there is not the same tradition of drinking perry as there is in England and Wales.

Styles of Cider

The various categories of cider mainly revolve around the level of sweetness, and different styles are suitable for different occasions.

Most cider is fermented to dryness, therefore sugar will be added to make sweet cider. A more natural way is to arrest fermentation before the yeast has converted all the sugar into alcohol. This will leave a low-strength sweet cider.

ARMAGH CIDER COMPANY

Kelly Troughton

**Ballinteggart House,
73 Drumnasoo Road,
Portadown, County Armagh
T: +44 (0)28 3833 4268
W: www.armaghcider.com
E: info@armaghcider.com**

County Armagh is known as 'the Orchard County' after the many orchards that are planted there. There is also a long tradition of farmhouse cidermaking in the orchard county but, as in the rest of Ireland, it died out over time. However, one family are changing that. The Armagh Cider Company is a family business started in 2005 and based at Ballinteggart House near Portadown. The Troughton family have lived in the house for over a hundred years and it was Thomas George Troughton, father of current owner Phillip, who planted the orchards. Indeed in the 1960s he had thought of making cider himself but the plans did not come to fruition.

Phillip had been thinking for a while how to add value to his crop – the orchard covers around 140 acres – so Armagh Cider was born, or maybe that should be re-born. Phillip's daughter Kelly is the main driving force behind the company and there has been some very positive early commercial success, following support by the local media and the Northern Ireland Department for Agriculture and Rural Development. Currently the cider is made in

England, using apples from the Ballinteggart orchard, but the plan has always been to bring production back to the farm. The successful early growth of the company means that cidermaking at Ballinteggart may happen sooner rather than later. In addition the acreage given over to orcharding is increasing. Orcharding recently increased from 100 acres to the current 140, with an extra planting of some dessert apples and the cider-apple varieties Michelin and Dabinett.

Currently, the company makes one cider but a mulled cider is available at Christmas time. As well as making cider they also make 'AJ' apple juice.

Availability

The cider is currently available in Northern Ireland with an especially strong presence in pubs, restaurants and off-licences in the counties of Armagh, Antrim and Down, as well as Belfast City. Expansion into the Republic of Ireland is the next goal. Carsons Cider is available in 330ml and 500ml bottles.

Visiting

Ballinteggart House is not open to the public.

CARSON'S CIDER

Sparkling dry cider
Alcohol: 4.8%

Carson was Philip's mother's maiden name and, to keep the name alive, he decided to use it to name the new cider. The dominant apple in the cider is the Bramley and it is joined by dessert apple varieties, Katy and Laxtons, and by Dabinett and Michelin cider apples.

The cider is clear and bright, having a straw-yellow colour. There is a good cidery aroma with culinary apples dominant on the nose and some tropical-fruit hints. The palate has a culinary apple sharpness with a nice level of acidity and tannin in the mouth-drying finish. Carsons is a decent, sharp and crisp dry cider, resulting in a very refreshing drink.

BULMERS/ MAGNERS

Annerville,
Clonmel,
County Tipperary
T: +353 (0)52 72100
W: www.bulmers.ie
(Republic of Ireland)
www.magners.com
(elsewhere)

One of the cider brands produced by Bulmers of Clonmel has been a phenomenon in Ireland and beyond. Known as 'Bulmers' in the Republic of Ireland and 'Magners' elsewhere, it is a huge success story and, in the process, has revolutionised the image of cider. Such has been the success that work has been proceeding at a fast pace to enable the Clonmel plant to keep up with the increasing demand.

Commercial cidermaking in Clonmel goes back to 1935 when William Magner started to produce cider at the old Murphy's Brewery in Dowd's Lane, closed since 1926. William Magner had some initial success, so much so that he attracted interest from over the water. A deal was done in March 1937, whereby the cidermaking side of Magner's business was turned into a separate company, with HP Bulmer of Herefordshire owning half of the shares. The brand 'Bulmers' was established and the business continued to flourish, selling up to two million gallons a year.

In 1946, HP Bulmer acquired the remaining shares from Magner, who eventually left the business in 1949. Under the Irish law of the time, a British company could not own an Irish one, so they arranged for an Irish national by the name of Thomas Jackson to be the owner of Bulmers in Ireland though HP Bulmer retained real overall control.

Competition between HP Bulmer

and their rivals in England – Showerings – shaped the next phase of the company. HP Bulmer eventually sold its shares to Thomas Jackson, so there now existed two companies with the right to use the Bulmer's name, one limited to Ireland and the other – HP Bulmer – with rights in all other markets. However, he was badly shaken by a car accident not long after the sale, and did not think he could run the business without the expertise of HP Bulmer. He sold the company to Showerings, who were owned by a consortium of Guinness and Allied Breweries, and in 1964 it became Showerings (Ireland). The Irish trademark for the name 'Bulmers' remained with this new company.

A huge expansion took place in 1965 when a new, modern production facility at Annerville, some three miles outside Clonmel, was opened by the then Taoiseach, Seán Lemass. Other brands were developed including Stag in 1974 and a perry called Ritz in 1986. However, the next significant development came in the late 1980s, when the decision was made to overhaul the image of Bulmers Cider in the Republic of Ireland.

The new marketing approach had great success, focusing on the quality of the product and its production in order to change people's attitudes to cider. The marketing campaign has delivered phenomenal growth for the Bulmers brand. In the early 1990s, Bulmers had less than a third of the cider market in Ireland. By 2003, it had more than 80 percent of that market, and total cider consumption in Ireland had quadrupled, fuelled by the Bulmers boom.

The next step was to launch the brand outside Ireland, but there was one hitch: the Bulmers name outside the Republic of Ireland remained the property of HP Bulmer of Herefordshire. So in 1999 the name 'Magners' was chosen, based on the original owner William Magner, and the product was launched outside the Republic of Ireland. With a similar marketing strategy, Magners has also become a huge success, with the plant in Clonmel just about managing to meet demand.

A huge investment has just taken place at Annerville to increase maturation and bottling capacity to meet this growing demand. Also, innovation continues apace with the launch of Bulmers Light in 2003 and the trialling of Bulmers Iced in the Republic of Ireland. Bulmers Iced is a draught cider but, instead of having to add ice cubes to serve over ice, part of the cider is frozen by the dispense system to form a head of iced cider. Sales of Magners continue to grow and the future looks very bright indeed for cidermaking at Clonmel.

Availability

Bulmers is widely available in the Republic of Ireland and, under the Magners label, is available in many countries worldwide – UK, Spain, Austria, Germany, Switzerland, Sweden, Finland, Netherlands, Belgium, Denmark, Portugal, Greece, Cyprus, Australia, Japan, the Canadian province of Ontario as well as in the following US states – New York, Massachusetts, California, New Jersey, Connecticut, Illinois, Maryland, Pennsylvania, Florida, Maine and Rhode Island. The other brands are available widely in the Republic of Ireland only.

Visiting

Neither Annerville nor Dowd's Lane are open to the public.

CIDERMAKING AT BULMERS

Production takes place at two sites – Dowd's Lane (the old Murphy's brewery) in the centre of Clonmel, and Annerville, three miles away.

Dowd's Lane is the historic site and many of the buildings are listed. Annerville is a much larger and more modern plant set in 250 acres of orcharding. Between the two, output from the 2005–06 harvest was 1 million hectolitres. This will be increased due to the extra capacity for maturation that has now been built at Annerville.

Apple crushing and fermentation takes place twenty-four hours a day, seven days a week during the harvest period, which starts in late summer and runs through to Christmas. One base cider is produced, which is then made-up as required to meet the specifications of the different brands being produced at Bulmers. As well as using their own apples, many growers throughout Ireland supply apples under contract, including a large quantity from County Armagh. A total of seventeen apple varieties go into the base cider, a mixture of dessert apples for sweetness, culinary apples for sharpness, and cider apples for tannin. The seventeen are – Michelin, Dabinett, Yarlington Mill, Bulmer's Norman, Tremlett's Bitter, Breakwells Seedling, Taylor's, Harry Master's Jersey, Medaille d'Or, Reine des Pommes, Ashton Bitter, Bramley, Grenadier, Brown Thorn, Brown Snout, Vilberie and Improved Dove. Dessert pears are used to make Ritz perry.

There is a beautiful smell of apples on arrival at Dowd's Lane. The apples are temporarily kept in two

ENJOY BULMERS SENSIBLY

The magic of a little ice

holding bays, one containing Bramleys and the other containing cider and dessert apples – Bramleys make up around half of the juice. The apples are washed in small channels from the bays – the apples float along the channels while any dirt and stones sink – until they are conveyed up to a hopper.

The pressing room in Dowd's Lane is a remarkable sight – men with leather aprons, overalls stained by apple juice, work at a furious pace, building cheeses and operating old hydraulic presses that have been there since HP Bulmer's time. The apples are milled as they descend from the hopper. Cheeses weighing one tonne each are constructed and stacked, after which juice begins to leak out due to the sheer weight of the cheeses above. The cheeses are given an initial press to get them into shape before the first real press brings forth a cascade of apple juice. The pomace is sent through another mill and

pressed again to extract any remaining juice. The pomace is now almost completely dry and leaves Dowd's Lane as animal feed.

The torrent of apple juice eventually drains into a storage vessel for analysis, and any treatments (such as chaptelisation, which is sometimes necessary to boost the level of sugar in the juice) is then considered. The juice is then pumped into the fermentation vats. The contrast between the frenzied activity of the pressing room and the cool, airy, atmospheric quiet of the fermentation hall with its massive oak vats could not be more marked. There are a number of huge vats of different sizes, some dating from 1936, with capacities ranging from 90 up to over 2,500 hectolitres. Each vat is filled to the brim and, remarkably for an industrial cider-maker, no yeast is added as it lives in the fabric of the plant, especially in the old oak vats. Although the yeast has been analysed

– it contains more than a hundred different strains – it has resisted culturing, and therefore no two fermentations will be exactly identical. As a result, skilled blending after maturation is required. Fermentation is at 18-24°C and generally lasts three to four weeks, although it can take longer late in the season when the ambient temperature is cooler.

The juice will be fermented to dryness and raw cider will spend around five to ten days on its lees – resting in the fermentation vat with the now dead yeast. The raw cider will be racked into a tanker and transported to Annerville for maturation. The maturation tanks are all insulated external tanks but are not temperature controlled. The raw cider will mature for between six and eighteen months, during which time it will be racked a second time by moving it from one maturation tank to another. Each tank will be regularly tested by a trained panel of tasters to assess the progress of the maturing cider. One of the things being assessed is the progress of the malo-lactic fermentation, which will have started in the fermentation vats. Once this is complete and the cider has matured, it will be deemed ready for a few final adjustments before packaging.

Base cider from different tanks will have matured differently, so they will be carefully blended before being filtered to remove any remaining residue. This blended base cider will then be made up depending on the specification of the final product it will become: sugar may be added to get the cider to the desired level of sweetness; potable water is added to adjust the level of alcohol downwards; acidity will be adjusted; and finally carbonation is increased. Although making-up will differ according to the final specification, the aim is to create a consistent product. The finished cider is then kegged, bottled or canned, with only some of the canned product being pasteurised.

Bulmers' main output is Bulmers/Magners cider, but it also makes a number of other cider products, and Ritz perry.

BULMERS/ MAGNERS
ORIGINAL CIDER
Sparkling medium sweet cider
Alcohol: 4.5%

Bulmers, or Magners as it is known outside the Republic of Ireland, is the flagship brand and is experiencing massive growth. It pours an orangey-amber colour and has a genuine cidery aroma. Also on the nose there

conscious. It has the same orangey-amber colour as Bulmers/Magners Original and the nose is similar but rather more muted. However, on the palate it is somewhat different, having a bitter-sweet quality associated with artificial sweeteners, and is rather thin in body. The finish has medium acidity and low tannin, making it a less characterful product than Bulmers/Magners Original.

is culinary apple, some woody notes and a hint of banana. In the mouth the cider is sweet, but has just enough balancing tannin on the somewhat short finish and a good degree of acidity. This is a cider clearly made to have a mass-market appeal but is nevertheless a quite refreshing and enjoyable medium-sweet cider.

STAG
Sparkling dry cider
Alcohol: 5.0%

Stag has been on the market since 1974 and is the only dry cider made by Bulmers. Dark gold in colour, it has a cider and culinary apple aroma with grapefruit and woody hints. The culinary apple comes through more in the mouth, joined by woody and citric qualities. Stag is fairly acidic and moderately tannic; making it a perfectly enjoyable dry cider.

BULMERS/ MAGNERS LIGHT

Sparkling light cider
Alcohol: 4.5%

Bulmers/Magners Light is a low calorie version of its namesake and is made to appeal to the calorie

product is similar to Linden Village in its target market.

LINDEN VILLAGE

Sparkling medium dry cider
Alcohol: 6.0%

Linden Village is one of the more basic brands made by Bulmers. There is very little on the nose apart from very light floral notes and some sulphur. The palate is dominated by a culinary apple tang while the finish has low tannin, moderate acidity and a certain harshness. Linden Village is a basic product appealing to a certain sector of the market.

RITZ

Sparkling medium sweet perry
Alcohol 4.7%

Ritz is the only perry made in Ireland and it has been on the market since 1986. Ritz is straw coloured and the nose is dominated by vanilla, with possibly a hint of tropical fruit lurking in the background. The palate is also vanilla dominated, sweet and the vanilla carries on through the moderately acidic finish. Ritz is an easy drinking and quite refreshing mass-market style of perry.

STRONGBOW

Sparkling medium dry cider
Alcohol: 6.0%

This cider is made by Bulmers and is not connected with the drink of the same name available in the UK and beyond. Strongbow has a fruity and vinous nose but also a noticeable presence of sulphur. Sweet and acidic on the palate and the finish is very short with a certain harsh quality. This rather thin and characterless

DOUBLE L CIDER

David Llewellyn in his orchard

Llewellyn's Orchard Produce, Quickpenny Road, Lusk, County Dublin
T: +353 (0)87 284 3879
E: pureapple@eircom.net

The beautiful and lush rolling countryside to the north of Dublin is the traditional fruit and vegetable growing area for the city and it is here that David Llewellyn makes his cider, Double L.

Fruit growing has long been a passion for David. He studied horticulture and worked in Germany as a fruit grower and winemaker. After moving back to Ireland, he began by renting land before buying his own greenfield site, on which he planted an apple orchard and vines.

His interest in winemaking and a realisation that no-one was making small scale farmhouse cider in Ireland led him to experiment. The result was Double L cider, which initially proved popular, but he unfortunately ran into difficulties with the excise.

However the problems are now resolved and Double L is again available for sale. The name 'Double L' comes from the numerous occasions David has had to spell his surname. It is a fine example of a real farmhouse cider with all the complexity such a product offers. In the future, David is even considering making a still cider.

David also produces a little wine and is well known in farmers' markets for his high quality fruit juices. He is also happy for people to bring their apples to him if they want them juiced.

Availability
Double L is available directly from David but only by the caseload, or at food and farmer's markets such as the Temple Bar Food Market, Dun Laoghaire Farmers Market and Red Stables Market in Clontarf.

Visiting
Pre-booked visits including tastings may be possible but must be arranged in advance.

MAKING DOUBLE L

Double L is made without compromising on naturalness and is a true farmhouse craft cider. Only Irish apples are used, most being David's own while a small quantity are bought from other apple growers. David's are handpicked, as he believes it leaves the apples sounder, cleaner and less bruised than mechanical harvesters. He has selected his apple varieties carefully so that he does not need to use any chemical sprays.

After milling the apples, he follows the traditional method of constructing cheeses which are then pressed to get the juice. He ferments in barrels or tanks using a German white wine yeast. Interestingly he does not always suppress the wild yeasts, instead allowing them to work with the wine yeast, making a most characterful and authentic finished cider.

Fermentation is not controlled but left to nature and can last anything from three weeks to six months, depending on the apple variety, time of year and the yeast that is at work. The cider is then racked and matured from six months to three years.

There is no 'making-up' as David does not want to compromise on the naturalness of the cider. The finished cider comes straight from the maturation vessels and is not filtered before bottling, meaning that a little yeast makes it into each bottle. He then adds a little apple juice to get a secondary fermentation in the bottle, creating a natural sparkling product without the need to add carbon dioxide. The presence of the yeast also makes Double L a real live cider that will be good for several years as it matures further in the bottle. Double L is a real cider made from nothing more than apple juice and yeast.

In addition to the two main products – Bone Dry and Dry Dabinett – David plans to make other single varietal ciders, such as Carmine and Elstar, from time to time depending on the season. Robust and fully flavoured, his ciders are a good accompaniment for strong cheeses such as mature cheddars.

BONE DRY

Style: Bottle-conditioned dry cider
Alcohol: around 6.5%

Bone Dry accounts for around two-thirds of David's cider production. It is made with the Dabinett cider apple, Bramley and a mix of dessert apples such as Katy, Jona Gold, Cox, Elstar and Carmine. The exact mix will depend on the season and availability. As David does not add

water to his cider to bring the alcohol level down to a fixed point, the alcoholic strength will vary depending on the fermentation and maturation conditions.

Depending on how long the bottle has been standing up, the cider will have a degree of haze, but a lengthy storage will make it drop almost bright. Bone Dry has a golden colour with a classic cidery aroma. The nose is highly complex and features pear-drops and some stewed-apple notes, possibly joined by some citrus and the leathery aroma that is a characteristic of wild yeast. Bottle-conditioning makes for a lightly sparkling cider, with fresh acidity from the Bramley and hints of earthiness, woodiness and a lemon sharpness. The finish is medium in tannin with good acidity and sharpness, generating an excellent quenching cider. This is cider unplugged and live, real cider – good, earthy, full of character and flavour, a million miles away from the sweet and fizzy mass-market style. As this is a farmhouse craft cider made in small batches, taste will vary by batch.

DRY DABINETT

Single varietal bottle conditioned dry cider
Alcohol: around 7.5%

Dry Dabinett is made from a single apple variety, the 'bittersweet' Dabinett cider apple – high in tannin but low in acid. The naturalness of the cidermaking process means that the alcoholic strength will vary.

As with Bone Dry, bottle-conditioning may make the cider slightly hazy but it is a deeper shade of gold – brownish-gold – than Bone Dry. There is a classic bittersweet, or cider apple, aroma with a spicy, herbal quality reminiscent of cloves and sage. The nose also reveals elderflower and orange notes. There is a quinine-tonic bitterness in the mouth, again lightly carbonated with a certain spiciness. The finish is assertive and long lasting with low acidity but high tannin, drying the mouth. To experience how a variety of cider apple can deliver a certain style of cider then this classic single varietal cider is a must-try. Another excellent and complex real cider from the Double L stable.

JOHNNY JUMP UP

Integrated Foods, Scariff, County Clare
Website currently under development, which will include contact details

Wilhelm Rost moved to beautiful east County Clare in 1986 and a year later he was making some cider in old whiskey barrels. Wilhelm is originally from northern Bavaria in Germany where fruit growing is a way of life. Making wine and cider is very much an integral part of the culture in that part of Germany and Wilhelm was himself a farmer in the region.
In 1987, he experimented by making some cider for himself in the old whiskey barrels and by 1991 he had begun to sell it. Initially he was able to sell the cider in some local pubs and in Galway. By 2001 he was exporting cider to Germany via his contacts there and had developed some connections to a drinks company in Finland who were importing the cider.

The recent upturn in consumption of cider has been a double-edged sword. On the one hand, the image of the drink has improved greatly, but it is very difficult for a small producer to compete against the mass marketing campaign of a big producer. Nevertheless he is hoping to expand sales into other European countries.

Availability
Johnny Jump Up Cider is available in bottle in certain parts of Ireland, especially in Cork County and City and in Galway, and is distributed by CR Drinks. It is also available in Germany and Finland.

Visiting
The cider mill is not open to the public.

Making Johnny Jump Up

Johnny Jump Up is made with fairly simple traditional methods using fully traceable ingredients. Output in a year is around 1400 hectolitres. The apples come from County Tipperary and Drogheda, County Louth.
After milling and pressing, the juice is fermented in stainless steel tanks for three to four months. Wilhelm uses a special single strain yeast that is recycled from fermentation to fermentation but also allows wild yeast to play a part in fermenting the juice. Some sweet apple juice concentrate from Italy is also used to balance the high acidity of Irish apples, this is fermented separately for six weeks.

The raw cider is then racked into maturation tanks. The length of maturation varies and young finished cider is carefully blended with older cider to keep the product fairly consistent from year to year. Nevertheless there will be some small variation year on year. After blending

the cider is filtered, the alcoholic strength is reduced by adding potable water and it is then taken to be bottled outside of Ireland. No artificial flavourings or chemicals are used during 'making up'. The cider is pasteurised in bottle and the carbonation adjusted.

JOHNNY JUMP UP

Sparkling medium dry cider
Alcohol: 4.5%

The name comes from a folk song written by Tadhg Jordan of Cork City in the 1940s. Apparently his friend was a pub landlord who asked him to write a song to increase the sales of cider in the bar. The song was later popularised by the famous Cork singer Jimmy Crowley.

Certainly not an ode to responsible drinking, but the humour of the song was the inspiration behind the naming of Johnny Jump Up.

Irish Bramley apples are the main variety, with some Carmine and Boskoop. It pours a golden colour and has a sweetish dessert apple aroma with grapefruit notes. More grapefruit follows on the palate and a mellow finish low in tannin but with decent acidity, making for an easy drinking medium dry cider.

NEW CIDER

**Mac's Cider, Barnhill
Orchards, Portadown,
County Armagh**
armaghcider@googlemail.com

A research-and-development project
on apple growing started by the
Department of Agriculture and Rural
Development in Northern Ireland has
borne fruit. The project researched
how apple growers could add value to
their crop. One of the outcomes of the
project was that County Armagh
apple growers could make farmhouse
craft cider.

A result of this project is Mac's
Cider, which has just been launched.
It is made from the apples of four
growers in County Armagh, though
more are welcome to join. The apples
are milled, pressed, fermented and
matured at Barnhill Orchards. This is
the first cider to be made in Northern
Ireland since World War II, and it
benefits from the 70 hectolitre duty
exemption granted by the British
government to small-scale
cidermakers in the UK. Currently
only a limited quantity is made in dry,
medium and sweet styles; it is
available at some farmers' markets in
Northern Ireland.

However, the future plans are
exciting indeed. The plan is to work
with the Irish Apple Collection so that
growers in County Armagh will be
able to use local apple varieties to
make their cider, giving it a regional
style. By doing this, it will be
possible to make 'Armagh Cider' a
protected geographical name, so that
only cider made in Armagh with local
apple varieties can use the
designation. It is hoped that in due
course County Armagh will become a
fully fledged cidermaking region,
with many small farmhouse-scale
producers making distinctive local
craft cider. Cidermaking is still in its
infancy in the Orchard County, but
hopefully it will soon reclaim its
rightful place as a cidermaking
region.

APPRECIATING BEER AND CIDER

Beer and cider are all too often dismissed as second-class products, to be drunk without much thought. However, beer and cider are amazingly complex products, easily as worthy of consideration and appreciation as any wine. In fact, the sheer range of styles that make up the beer family provide a spectrum of aroma and flavour far greater than that found in wines.

Glassware

To appreciate beer and cider good glassware is essential, a large tulip-shaped red-wine glass will do the trick as the bowl is perfect for swirling the drink to release its aromas. The glass must be scrupulously clean as any detergent residue will affect the flavour of the drink and kill the head on beer. Finally, hold the glass by the stem as the human hand will quickly warm any beer.

Temperature

The correct temperature at which to serve a beer is crucial to appreciating the different styles. Ales and stouts are generally best at around 12°C – cellar temperature. Depending on the fridge, thirty to sixty minutes' chilling should suffice: too cold and the complex aromas will be lost. Wheat beer should be slightly colder, around 10°C, and may take two to three hours in the fridge. Lager should be served cold as it is meant to be clean, crisp and refreshing. To get it to the 6-8°C range will take four to five hours of refrigeration, or even better leave it in the fridge overnight.

Cider is somewhat more flexible and is often drunk at lager temperatures. However, to appreciate a complex cider, ale temperatures are best to unleash the fullness of the aroma.

Tasting Conditions

Good light and the absence of strong odours are a must. Good light will allow for the appreciation of the subtle colours of the drink. Strong odours such as perfume, aftershave, cooking, cigarette smoke and so on will all mask the aromas and must be avoided. Water and plain crackers are good for cleansing the palate between drinks.

TASTING BEER AND CIDER

If tasting different styles of beer, start with the lightest in flavour and build up. Fill the large red wine glass to around halfway and then ake it step by step. Cider should be tasted from sweet to dry or vice versa.

Appearance

Note the colour of the beer and the formation of the head: is it dense, rocky, billowing? The colour of cider can go from white with little colour to a reddish-brown. The darker the cider, the more tannic it is likely to be, but this may be distorted by the use of colouring by large-scale cidermakers.

Aroma

Swirl the drink in the glass and sniff. Does the beer exhibit aromas associated with malt: coffee, chocolate, biscuit, malt or toffee? Hops will be detected by floral, citric, peppery, spicy, resiny, herbal overtones while some fruitiness may be due to the yeast strain. Cider should be 'cidery' and smell of apples whilst perry should smell of pears, but there will be a wide range of other aromas found in well-made cider. Other fruity aromas such as tropical fruits, berries, summer fruits, dried fruit and citrus will come from esters. Cider can also exhibit floral, perfumy characteristics as well as grassiness and nuttiness. Vanilla, honey and toffee can also be detected and traditional cider apples will impart spicy and woody notes.

Taste

Is the beer sweet, bitter, malty? How does it feel in the mouth? The main thing to look for in a cider is its sweetness and acidity – detected by how much it makes your mouth water after swallowing.

Finish

Does the beer finish by drying the mouth and give further hop characteristics? Is there a refreshing and more-ish bitterness? A good beer makes you want more and its flavour lingers in the mouth. Does the cider dry and pucker the mouth, suggesting tannins.

Assessment

Did the beer live up to its style and was it complex or simply bland? Lagers should be crisp and clean, and have a good floral or grassy hop bouquet and a delicate, but noticeable, drying bitterness in the finish. Good ales will be fruity and complex with the malty sweetness balanced by a good level of hop bitterness in the finish. Stouts will be roasty and have a coffee or chocolate character with a firm drying bitter finish possibly with a sour tang. Wheat beers will be fruity or herbal and have a tart, refreshing finish. Was the cider complex or just bland sweet alcoholic apple juice? A good cider has a depth of aroma and flavour and is very refreshing.

POURING BEER

It is a myth that a beer with a big head is a sign of incompetence on the part of the pourer. In fact, it is a sign of ignorance on the part of the critic. Each beer style needs to be poured carefully to maximise its character. The head of the beer contains hop oils and aroma compounds. Try tasting the head on its own – it is not pleasant.

Stout

Bottled stout needs to be poured slowly as the head will develop quickly. Pour in two stages: pause about three-quarters of the way, allow the head to die down a bit and then finish off. This will give the stout a dense, solid, rocky head. Stouts with widgets and nitrogenated draught stout give a thick creamy head but lack the flavour of bottled stout.

Ale

Ales can be poured a bit more quickly and as you straighten the glass you should be looking to end up with a head about as thick as a finger.

Lager

Like stout, the best lagers can be poured in two stages. For the first stage, keep the glass tilted an angle and pour until the beer reaches the rim. Then, after the head has settled somewhat, pour the remainder of the beer with the glass vertical. The end result should be a two-finger thickness of foam with the head rising over the rim of the glass like an ice cream. To get a two-finger

thickness of foam on lesser lagers will require a vigorous pour.

Wheat beer

Wheat beers need to be poured gently because the presence of wheat generates a big head. With unfiltered wheat beer, drinkers stop when the bottle is almost empty, swirl the remaining contents and dump it into the beer. This gets all the yeast into the beer, making it very cloudy. Wheat beers should have a billowing head of foam rising well above the glass.

Bottle-conditioned beer and cider

Bottle-conditioned beer and cider will contain a sediment of yeast and therefore should be stood upright for a good few hours – overnight is best – before pouring to allow the sediment to fall to the bottom. Bottle-conditioned beer needs to be poured slowly as the presence of yeast in the bottle can cause a strong carbonation and too much head if not handled correctly. Pour under a strong light so that, as you get towards the end of the bottle, the sediment will appear in the neck of the bottle. For a bright and clear product, pouring has to stop and the remainder decanted. The sediment is, however, harmless and is rich in minerals – some drinkers are known to put it into a shot glass as a tonic.

BEST BEER BARS AND PUBS IN IRELAND

CONNACHT

Bierhaus

2 Henry Street, Galway City
T: +353 (0)91 587 766
W: www.bierhausgalway.ie
E: bierhausgalway@gmail.com

Based in what some would describe as the 'bohemian' part of Galway, the Bierhaus caters for a discerning clientele always on the lookout for a new beer experience. An open plan, modern looking bar, it is owned and run by three young Galwegians with a passion for beer. There is a good draught range featuring the local brew, Galway Hooker, as well as O'Hara's stout from Carlow with German lagers and wheat beers. The Bierhaus also has a very impressive bottle range with a large quantity of Belgian beer, German wheat beers and lagers as well as Polish beer, supplemented with other international brews, all on a handy menu. The Bierhaus is a lively spot and gets livelier at weekends with a DJ to entertain the punters.

Sheridan's on the Dock

3 New Dock, Galway City
T: +353 (0)91 564 905

Owned by Seamus Sheridan of Sheridan's Cheesemongers fame, the same philosophy is applied to the pub as to his other ventures – quality. Sheridan's has a nice, relaxed, vaguely Mediterranean feel and sits right on the docks in Galway. There is a good draught selection, featuring Galway Hooker, O'Hara's stout from Carlow brewery, Kinsale Irish Lager with some wheat beers and a continental lager. The bottled list is impressive and has a good Belgian and British selection with a featured beer of the week. Interesting cider is also on the menu, including Johnny Jump Up and some excellent English offerings. As well as the beer, there is some excellent food and wine available, the bar is exactly what would be expected from someone at the forefront of the slow food movement.

LEINSTER

Bull and Castle

5-7 Lord Edward Street, Christ Church, Dublin 2
T: +353 (0)1 475 1122
W: www.bullandcastle.ie
E: info@bullandcastle.ie

The Bull and Castle describes itself as Ireland's only gastro pub and is part of the FXB chain of steak and seafood restaurants, where the food is all free range and farm-traceable. There has been a pub here for a long time and was, until recently, known as the Castle Inn. This pub was one of the first in Dublin to sell draught Guinness, due to its proximity to St James's Gate brewery. The beer menu contains a long list of excellent Czech and German lagers, English ales, Belgian beers, German wheat beers and much, much more. But what really makes the Bull and Castle special is the food menu in which each wholesome dish is accompanied by a matching beer and some dishes have beer as an ingredient. The Bull and Castle has a relaxed, informal and friendly atmosphere with knowledgeable staff who are passionate about their beer and spirits and see it as part of their mission to educate people about the joys of beer. There is also a good Irish whiskey menu as well as other whiskeys and premium spirits. Upstairs is a Bavarian-style beer hall complete with long tables; beer is available in one-litre steins.

Messrs Maguires

1 & 2 Burgh Quay, Dublin 2
T: +353 (0)1 670 5777

This brewpub near O'Connell Bridge has already been featured but the bar itself also deserves a mention. This popular bar is spread over three levels and much of the original decorative features have been restored. For beer lovers, the main point of interest is the house-brewed beers Rusty and Weiss, as well as the three changing brews, one being either the Pils or Haus lagers, one being a type of stout or porter and the other a different style of lager.

The Porterhouse

The Porterhouse Bray, Strand Road, Bray County Wicklow
T: +353 (0)1 286 0668
The Porterhouse Central, 45-47 Nassau Street, Dublin 2
T: +353 (0)1 677 4180
Porterhouse North
Cross Guns Bridge, Glasnevin, Dublin 9
T: +353 (0)1 830 9884
The Porterhouse Temple Bar
16-18 Parliament Street, Dublin 2
T: +353 (0)1 679 8847
W: www.porterhousebrewco.com
E: info@porterhousebrewco.com

As well as brewing, the Porterhouse also operate four pubs in the Dublin area and even one in London's Covent Garden. Although they are all different, there is one overarching theme – quality beer. Not only do they offer their own excellent beers on draught, including seasonal specialities, but they also have a huge selection of bottled beers from all over the world. The original Porterhouse is in Bray and also offers accommodation, with each room named after a beer. The popular Porterhouse Temple Bar has a great pub feel and character and is found just off Grattan Bridge. The two newest pubs are Porterhouse North, in an old art deco garage in Glasnevin with a beer garden attached, and Porterhouse Central, right in the heart of Dublin on Nassau Street. The Porterhouse also runs a number of beer festivals throughout its outlets during the year. All venues serve food and often have live music.

MUNSTER

....

Biddy Early

Inagh, Ennis, County Clare
T: +353 (0)65 683 6742
W: www.beb.ie, E: info@beb.ie

Biddy Early is a good country pub made even better by the fact it brews its own beer. As well as its own excellent brews, including seasonals, it has a good range of bottled beer from all over the world, from Belgian trappist ales to Japanese lager. There is also a restaurant which follows the Biddy Early philosophy of sourcing locally – the food is all as local as possible and they even bake their own bread. So when visiting the Cliffs of Moher or the Burren, a stop at Biddy Early's should also be on the itinerary.

The Bierhaus

Popes Quay, Cork City
T: +353 (0)21 455 1648
E: thebierhaus.corkcity@hotmail.com

The Bierhaus in Cork is not connected to its namesake in Galway but has a similar approach when it comes to beer. It is a bright glass-fronted bar with a modern interior and comfy couches sitting right on the northern channel of the River Lee. Friar Weiss and Rebel Red from the Franciscan Well Brewery just down the road are available on draught, as are Hoegaarden, Krombacher and Staroprammen, together with a changing guest draught beer. The beer menu features excellent beers from Belgium, Germany, Eastern Europe and beyond.

The Franciscan Well

14 North Mall, Cork City
T: +353 (0)21 421 0130
W: www.franciscanwellbrewery.com
E: info@franciscanwellbrewery.com

The brewery has a pub attached with a great beer garden out the back. The pub serves their own five great regular draught beers, three of them directly from 13.5 hectolitre tanks behind the bar, as well as a changing seasonal speciality. Also, they frequently serve a cask-conditioned version of their own beer or a guest, as well as having a decent selection of imported bottled beers such as Schneider Weisse, the Scottish Fraoch and other herb beers and beers from the Watou Brewery in Belgium. The Franciscan Well organise two beer excellent beer festivals each year at Easter and October.

Harbour Bar

Silly, Kinsale
T: +353 (0)21 477 2528

The Harbour Bar in Kinsale is aptly named as it overlooks the beautiful harbour. A small, homely and old-fashioned place, it is pretty unique in not having any draught beer. The bar has never had any draught beer and current owner Timothy Platt wants to keep it that way. The bottled beer selection is, however, excellent – German wheat beers and lagers, English ales, Belgian beer and Czech lagers are among the delights on offer here.

Mutton Lane Inn

St Patrick's Street, Cork City
T: +353 (0)21 427 3471

One of the oldest pubs in Cork can be found down a small alleyway – Mutton Lane – just off St Patrick's Street in the heart of Cork City. The pub is so named because it is built on the lane through which sheep were driven to the English Market. The owner is Benny McCabe, who owns two other pubs in Cork city. Benny loves beer and is on a mission to save the Irish pub, being concerned about how many are now turning into 'bars'. The Mutton Lane Inn is a small, cosy and busy traditional pub with a good beer menu featuring Belgian trappist beers as well as some from the UK, Germany, Eastern Europe and beyond.

The Oval

25 South Main Street, Cork City
T: +353 (0)21 427 7406

The Oval sits opposite the entrance to the Beamish and Crawford Brewery and, if Cork folklore is to be believed, the Beamish tap is directly connected to the Brewery. True or not, it certainly serves a good pint of Beamish. The pub was substantially rebuilt in 1919 in the Charles Rennie Mackintosh style and is about to become a listed building. The Oval is another of Benny McCabe's pubs and has the same great beer menu as Mutton Lane Inn.

Sin É

8 Coburg Street, Cork City
T: +353 (0)21 450 2266

Sin É is Irish for 'that's it' and is the third of Benny McCabe's pubs with the same beer menu as the Mutton Lane Inn and The Oval. The Sin É is a small, intimate bar often hosting traditional-music sessions. It draws a very mixed crowd of anything from country folk and locals to students. It bizarrely had a barber shop upstairs for a good while, but the funeral parlour next door has created some hair-raising moments of a different kind, as unsuspecting customers have heard the Rosary being recited through the walls of the men's toilets.

Tara's Speciality Beer House

Main Street, Ballina/Killaloe, County Tipperary
T: +353 (0)61 374777
E: agreatpint@hotmail.com

On the Tipperary side of the twin villages of Ballina and Killaloe is a real gem for the beer lover. Tara's Speciality Beer House is a very friendly and welcoming pub that is popular with both locals and tourists. It has a huge selection of bottled beer from all over the world and a few English ciders. The menu is so big – over seventy beers and ciders – that it is spread across several blackboards throughout the pub. As well as the bottled range, they have a cask-conditioned beer on draught, usually supplied by Messrs Maguires. There is a small bar, and an unconnected bigger lounge – entrances are through separate doors – and a beer garden, making this a great place to enjoy beer. The pub also hosts two beer festivals in February and July
each year.

ULSTER

Bittles Bar

70, Upper Church Lane, Belfast
T: +44 (0)28 9031 1088

One of the smallest bars in Belfast but with one of the largest selections of bottled beer. The triangular red brick end of terrace building, near the courts and the new Victoria Square development, has been a pub for around a hundred and fifty years and the current owner John Bittles has been there almost twenty years. John keeps a range of wheat beers, stouts, lagers, English ales and ciders, Trappist beers and more in this popular local bar. There is an Irish literary theme with paintings on the walls. Bittles also has a whiskey menu.

The Crown Liquor Saloon

46 Great Victoria Street, Belfast
T: +44 (0)28 9027 9901
W: www.crownbar.com
E: info@crownbar.com

One of the most beautiful bars in the world, both outside and in, a Victorian gem that has remained unchanged in a century. Marble work and stained glass on the outside; ornate woodwork, etched glass, a mosaic-tiled floor, amongst other features, on the inside. The Crown is so special that it is owned by the conservation body, the National Trust. A particular feature of the Crown is that seating is confined to ten snugs, each having its own door opening into the main bar. With the door closed, the booths are totally private and the bar keeps it that way, with staff only going in to clean. The tradition is that if the door to the booth is open anyone is welcome to come in, but if closed it means the occupants want to be left in private. The Crown is synonymous with Belfast and dates back to 1826, when it was called the Railway Tavern. It still attracts the locals and a good proportion of tourists. There are three cask-conditioned ales on offer, all from the Whitewater Brewery. Belfast Ale is joined by Crown and Glory, a brew unique to the Crown, and a third ale whose identity changes over the year. The Crown is one of the must-see pubs in the world and not to be missed.

The Dirty Duck Ale House

2-4 Kinnegar Road, Holywood, County Down
T: +44 (0)28 9059 6666
W: www.thedirtyduckalehouse.co.uk
E: comments@thedirtyduckalehouse.co.uk

On the shores of Belfast Lough with a great view across to County Antrim, The Dirty Duck is over a hundred years old and has had many name changes in that time. The bar itself is compact but there is also a restaurant upstairs and a beer garden. The owner, Mark McCrory, used to distribute cask-conditioned ales to pubs across Northern Ireland, but now concentrates on selling good ale in his own pub. There are usually three ales available at anyone time, sometimes joined by a fourth. Once an ale is finished a new one takes its place, meaning that the pub has about thirty different ales a month. The majority tend to be from Great Britain but Belfast's College Green beers may also be found there. The pub runs a weekly Ale Club and organises a beer festival during the summer.

Hillside

21 Main Street, Hillsborough, County Down
T: +44 (0)28 9268 2765

The Hillside is aptly named located halfway up the hill in the beautiful village of Hillsborough in County Down. The green fronted pub usually has three cask-conditioned ales available, which are a mixture of Whitewater Brewery's beers and those from England. Recently it has expanded into bottled ales, featuring those from the excellent St Peter's Brewery in England. Whitewater's Blonde lager and Aspall cider are also available. The Hillside is a real pub which is geared around socialising, having no TV, gaming machines or jukebox, and there is also an excellent restaurant. A beer festival is organised in the courtyard during the summer and the pub also hosts a popular oyster festival on the first weekend in September.

JD Wetherspoon

The Spinning Mill, 17-20 Broughshane Road, Ballymena
T: +44 (0)2825 638 985
The Bridge House, 35-43 Bedford Street, Belfast
T: +44 (0)2890 727890
The Central Bar, 13-15 High Street, Carrickfergus
T: +44 (0)2893 357 840
The Old Courthouse, Castlerock Road, Coleraine
T: +44 (0)2870 325 820
The Diamond, 23-24 The Diamond, Derry/Londonderry
T: +44 (0)2871 272880
The Ice Wharf, 22-24 Strand Road, Derry/Londonderry
T: +44 (0)2871 276 610
The Linen Hall, 11-13 Townhall Street, Enniskillen
T: +44 (0)2866 340 910
The Tuesday Bell, Lisburn Square, Lisburn
T: +44 (0)2892 627 390
The Spirit Merchant, 54-56 Regent Street, Newtownards
T: +44 (0)2891 824270

JD Wetherspoon is a chain of pubs that operates throughout the UK. The Bridge House in Belfast and the Ice Wharf in Derry/Londonderry are part of a different brand called Lloyds No1 and tend to be livelier and noisier, but are operated by the same company. They own a number of bars in Northern Ireland but tend to be large in size and offer very good value prices for both drinks and food. Each bar has a selection of cask-conditioned ales, mainly Scottish, as well as a selection of global lagers and some English real cider and perry.

The John Hewitt

51 Donegall Street, Belfast
T: +44 (0)28 9023 3768
W: www.thejohnhewitt.com
E: info@thejohnhewitt.com

The pub is found in Belfast's up and coming Cathedral Quarter and is relatively new. It is quite unique in being owned and run by the Belfast Unemployed Resource Centre, an organisation dedicated to combating unemployment and campaigning against the effects of poverty. Owning the pub generates income for the centre and provides employment and skills for some of the local unemployed. John Hewitt was a Belfast poet of note and, although he did not drink himself, he was politically left-leaning and opened the Unemployed Resource Centre. Pedro Donald manages the bar and he convinced the owners that they should go for a diverse beer selection. Two cask-conditioned ale are available usually from Hilden or College Green, though sometimes from other independent breweries in Britain. Erdinger and Hoegaarden wheat beers and Bitburger Pils are also available on draught. There is a good bottled beer selection supplemented by two guests, one of which will be an ale. Though new, The John Hewitt has a traditional feel – no TV, no gambling machines – and a relaxed atmosphere drawing an artistic, 'bohemian' crowd. It hosts many events and has a diverse live music scene – anything from traditional Irish music, Ulster Scots folk, jazz, Cajun and more. The walls are covered with the works of local artists, all of which can be purchased, the bar taking no commission, making for an ever changing décor.

White Horse Inn

49-53 Main Street, Saintfield, County Down
T: +44 (0)28 9751 1143

The White Horse Inn is owned and run by Bernard Sloan of the Whitewater Brewery, but the pub itself dates back well over two hundred years. As an outlet for the brewery, it stocks Whitewater's lager as well as the cask-conditioned ales. There are five cask ales normally available, being a mix of Whitewater's own beers and others from Great Britain. The White Horse has a relaxed and comfortable feel with a modern-style interior. There is excellent food to be had both in the pub and the Oast Restaurant, while a beer festival is held early in the year.

BEER FESTIVAL CALENDAR

FEBRUARY

Tara's Speciality Beer House Beer Festival

Tara's Speciality Beer House, Main Street, Ballina/Killaloe, County Tipperary

The pub has a vast range of beer but also organises two annual beer festivals. The first has a theme – such as Belgian beer – that changes annually. The festival usually takes place during the last week of February but it is advisable to check in advance.

T: +353 (0)61 374777
E: agreatpint@hotmail.com

MARCH

Porterhouse Stout Festival

The Porterhouse Bray, Strand Road, Bray County Wicklow
The Porterhouse Central, 45-47 Nassau Street, Dublin 2

Porterhouse North, Cross Guns Bridge, Glasnevin, Dublin 9
The Porterhouse Temple Bar, 16-18 Parliament Street, Dublin 2
The Porterhouse runs a number of beer festivals throughout the year across their pubs. The dates and themes of these festivals change each year but will each have a special beer brewed to match the occasion. As well as these festivals, there are two set dates: the Stout Festival taking place around St Patrick's Day, with a Chocolate Truffle Stout as the special brew, and the Oktoberfest, in the autumn.

(Bray) T: +353 (0)1 286 0668
(Central) T: +353 (0)1 677 4180
(North) T: +353 (0)1 830 9884
(Temple Bar) T: +353 (0)1 679 8847
W: www.porterhousebrewco.com
E: info@porterhousebrewco.com

White Horse Inn Beer Festival

White Horse Inn, 49-53 Main Street, Saintfield, County Down

Usually held over a weekend around St Patrick's Day. The pub already has five cask-conditioned ales available and these are supplemented by a separate bar with more ales from all over Britain. The date of the festival is not fixed so it is advisable to check well in advance.

T: +44 (0)28 9751 1143

EASTER

Franciscan Well Easterfest

The Franciscan Well, 14 North Mall, Cork City

One of two beer festivals organised by the Franciscan Well Brewery each year. Easterfest offers a chance to sample the products of Irish craft brewing with each brewery invited to have its own mini bar in the beer garden.

T: +353 (0)21 421 0130
W: www.franciscanwellbrewery.com
E: info@franciscanwellbrewery.com

JUNE

Hillside Beer Festival

Hillside, 21 Main Street, Hillsborough, County Down

The three handpumps in the pub are joined by another six in the courtyard. This means that there are ten cask-conditioned ales available at any given time over the weekend. Joining the Whitewater beers are those from breweries all over Britain. Tasting sessions are also a feature of this festival. The festival does not have a fixed date but is held over a weekend in June and it is therefore advisable to check in advance.
T: +44 (0)28 9268 2765

JULY

Tara's Speciality Beer House Bee Festival

Tara's Speciality Beer House, Main Street, Ballina/Killaloe, County Tipperary

This is the second beer festival held in this great pub and coincides with the Féile Brian Boru held in Ballina and Killaloe in the middle of July. The theme for this beer festival is usually Irish beer.
T: +353 (0)61 374777
E: agreatpint@hotmail.com

AUGUST

Kerry Beer Tasting Festival

D. O'Shea's Bar, North Square, Sneem, County Kerry

The last weekend in August is the time for the Kerry Beer Tasting Festival centred on O'Shea's Bar in Sneem. Many cask-conditioned ales from Irish craft brewers are available as well as a good range of Polish beers. Bottled beer comes from all over – England, USA, Russia – and there are also Irish and English ciders available.
T: +353 (0)64 45515
W: www.sneem.com/beerfestival.html

Hilden Beer Festival

Hilden Brewery, Grand Street, Hilden, Lisburn, Co. Antrim

Also on the last weekend in August is the Hilden Beer Festival, a long-running and very popular event held in the brewery's courtyard and featuring live music and good food. The brewhouse becomes a bar, serving Hilden's ales as well as other cask-conditioned brews from the rest of the UK and some from Irish craft brewers.
T: +44 (0)2892 660800
W: www.hildenbrewery.co.uk
E: irishbeers@hildenbrewery.co.uk

Dirty Duck Beer Festival

The Dirty Duck Ale House, 2-4 Kinnegar Road, Holywood, County Down

This festival is usually held towards the end of August or early September so it is advisable to check in advance. An extra bar is set up in the beer garden to serve the best cask-conditioned ale possible.

T: +44 (0)28 9059 6666
W: www.thedirtyduckalehouse.co.uk
E: comments@thedirtyduckalehouse.co.uk

OCTOBER

Franciscan Well Octoberfest

The Franciscan Well, 14 North Mall, Cork City

Held over the last weekend in October, this is the second of two beer festivals organised by the Franciscan Well Brewery each year. Octoberfest focuses on imported beers with a large range available over the weekend.

T: +353 (0)21 421 0130
W: www.franciscanwellbrewery.com
E: info@franciscanwellbrewery.com

Porterhouse Octoberfest

The Porterhouse Bray, Strand Road, Bray County Wicklow
The Porterhouse Central, 45-47 Nassau Street, Dublin 2
Porterhouse North, Cross Guns Bridge, Glasnevin, Dublin 9
The Porterhouse Temple Bar, 16-18 Parliament Street, Dublin 2

The second of the Porterhouse set beer festivals. A Kölsch-style beer is brewed for the festival and a number of bottled German beers are available. The festival takes place across the Porterhouse pubs.

(Bray) T: +353 (0)1 286 0668
(Central) T: +353 (0)1 677 4180
(North) T: +353 (0)1 830 9884
(Temple Bar) T: +353 (0)1 679 8847

W: www.porterhousebrewco.com
E: info@porterhousebrewco.com

NOVEMBER

Belfast Beer and Music Festival

Ulster Hall, Bedford Street, Belfast

The biggest of them all and organised by the Northern Ireland branch of Camra – the Campaign for Real Ale. It is held in the large Ulster Hall in the centre of the city and features over a hundred cask-conditioned ales from throughout the British Isles and a great deal of still real ciders and perries. Add to this live music, food and traditional pub games and it makes for a great weekend's entertainment. The festival tends to be held during the middle of November but it is worth checking in advance to find the precise date.

T: +44 (0)28 9032 3900 (Ulster Hall Box Office)
W: www.ulsterhall.co.uk and www.camrani.org.uk
E: ulsterhall@belfastcity.org.uk

A to Z of the Best Imported Beers

1698

Shepherd Neame Brewery, Faversham, Kent, England
Bottle-conditioned strong ale,
Alcohol: 6.5%

Shepherd Neame is located in the heart of East Kent's hop country. It is Britain's oldest surviving brewer, having been founded back in 1698. The brewery was owned by the Shepherd family for a large part of its history. They were then joined by the Neame's, which gave the brewery its present name. Although the Shepherd family are no longer connected to the brewery, it is still family-owned with the fifth generation of the Neame family currently at the helm. This beer was originally brewed as a celebration ale in 1998 to mark the brewery's tercentenary. It is a dark amber brew with an unmistakable aroma of pear drops, fruit and malt. More pears, malt and fruit on the palate with warming alcohol in the not overly hoppy finish which is joined by the return of the pear drops. 1698 is an excellent bottle-conditioned ale and one to savour. Distributed by Noreast Beers.

ASPALL DRAUGHT SUFFOLK CYDER

Aspall Hall, Debenham, Suffolk, England
Medium dry sparkling cider,
Alcohol: 5.5%

Aspall Cyder has been owned and managed by the Chevallier family since 1728, when Clement Chevallier decided to made some Normandy style cider in his stately home – Aspall Hall. Things really took off in the 1970s under John Chevallier who turned the operation into a real business, adding apple juice and cider vinegar to the portfolio of products. The cider is blended from a variety of base ciders and has to pass a tasting panel that has at least one member of the family in attendance. Aspall Draught is yellowish-green in colour with a bouquet of fragrant apple accompanied by banana notes. Sharp and crisp in the mouth with a little tannin and a moderate degree of acidity on the finish. This is a lovely cider, or should that be cyder, that would be a good replacement for white wine at any meal. Distributed by Noreast Beers.

ASPALL DRY PREMIER CRU

Aspall Hall, Debenham, Suffolk, England
Dry sparkling cider, Alcohol: 7.0%

Henry and Barry Chevallier currently manage the business which goes back eight generations. The Premier Cru is a pale yellow cider with a fresh and fruity nose of fragrant orange with hints of cinnamon. There is also a detectable solvent-like quality and some blackcurrant aroma in this very complex product. On the palate the cider is citric and uncompromisingly dry. The finish is initially bone dry until the acidity is felt and that blackcurrant quality returns. This is an excellent dry cider and would give a Sauvignon Blanc a run for its money.
Distributed by Noreast Beers.

BISHOPS FINGER

Shepherd Neame Brewery, Faversham, Kent, England
English Bitter,Alcohol: 5.4%

The beer is named after ancient signposts in the area that featured a clenched hand and one finger pointing pilgrims in the right direction to Canterbury. The style of signpost can still be found in the area. This Bishop's Finger is a 'best bitter', stronger than a regular bitter and is brewed using local malt and hops. Dark amber in colour with a reddish tinge, it has a wonderful malty nose of rich dark fruits. The palate is fruity with a degree of roastiness and some tangy hops. The finish is roasty and lingering, making for an excellent, robust and fully flavoured bitter.
Distributed by Noreast Beers.

BITBURGER

Bitburger Braugruppe, Bitburger Brauerei, Bitburg, German
German Pilsner-style lager, Alcohol: 4.8%

'Bitte ein Bit' is a well-known slogan in Germany – meaning 'a Bit please' – and the beer to which it refers, Bitburger, is just as well-known outside its home country. The brewery began as a farmhouse concern with the Simon family becoming owners soon after it was established. They still own the brewery today. Bitburger was possibly the first German brewery to use the term 'pilsner' to describe its golden lager beer – naming its product 'Simonbräu-Deutsch-Pilsner'. However brewers from the Czech city of Plzen – Pilsen in German – took them to court, arguing that only a beer from that city could use the term Pilsner. The German court ruled that 'pilsner' denoted a style of beer rather than an appellation of origin. However, the court declared that brewers must nevertheless put the beer's place of origin on the label to eliminate any confusion between pilsners brewed in Pilsen and those brewed elsewhere. Simonbräu changed its name to Bitburger Pilsener, after the small town of Bitburg in which it is brewed, eventually changing to Bitburger Pils to further eliminate any confusion. Other German brewers did likewise, adding the name of their hometown to the designation 'Pils'. Bitburger is a straw-coloured beer with a perfumy aroma and a tangy hop palate. The finish is dry with a long-lasting bitterness. Bitburger is an excellent pils in the drier German style.
Distributed by Blaney Wines.

BLANCHE DE NAMUR

Brasserie du Bocq, Purnode, Belgium
Belgian-style wheat beer, Alcohol: 4.5%

This Belgian-style wheat beer is made by the traditional Brasserie du Bocq, named after a local river. Brewing began back in 1858 by Martin Bellot, a farmer who brewed beer in the winter months. Success came after the First World War with an ale by the name of La Gauloise, so much so that farming became a secondary concern and eventually ceased in 1960. The brewery is currently run by the sixth generation of the family and makes a range of interesting beers. Blanche de Namur, in typical Belgian style, is spiced with coriander and bitter orange peel and bottled with a thick layer of yeast. It pours a hazy pale straw colour and has a bouquet bursting with citrus fruit alongside some spiciness and yeastiness in the background. The palate and finish are very citric and tart, making for a supremely refreshing drink. Blanche de Namur is a superb beer, packed with flavour and an excellent example of the Belgian style of wheat beer.
Distributed by Blaney Wines

BUDWEISER BUDVAR

Budějovicky Pivovar, České Budějovice, Czech Republic
Budweiser lager, Alcohol: 5.0%

In the Czech Republic a pilsner can only come from Plzen and therefore a 'budweiser' can only come from Budweis, the German name for the Czech city of Budějovice. The Budweiser style is distinct from those of Plzen, being mellower and less hoppy. Budvar is short for Budějovicky Pivovar, the brewery's name and therefore denotes a Budweiser beer made by Budvar. Its American namesake was actually brewed before Budvar started in 1895 but there were other brewers in the town long before that date, using the generic term 'Budweiser' for their beers. Indeed, it was the popularity of the beers from Budweis that made Anheuser-Busch use the term for its light lager. Budvar is far more flavoursome than its American namesake, partly due to the fact that it is an all-malt brew while the American version uses a large quantity of rice as an adjunct. Budvar pours a full gold colour and has a light floral aroma. There is a light, spicy hoppiness on the palate with a delicate bitterness on the finish. An enjoyable lager that is true to the name 'Budweiser'.
Distributed by Noreast Beers.

ERDINGER WEISSBIER

Privatbrauerei Erdinger Weissbrau, Erding, Germany
South German unfiltered wheat beer
Alcohol: 5.3%

Erdinger was founded in 1886 and is now the largest wheat beer brewery in the world, indeed it brews nothing else. The signature beer is Erdinger 'mit feine hefe' which translates as 'with fine yeast'. It pours a cloudy gold and has an aroma of bubblegum, apple and sherbet. The palate is light and fruity with a mild yeasty bite. There is a mild bitterness and tartness in the fruity finish. Erdinger is one of the most delicate interpretations of the style.
Distributed by Noreast Beers.

ERDINGER WEISSBIER DUNKEL

Privatbrauerei Erdinger Weissbrau, Erding, Germany
South German dark unfiltered wheat beer
Alcohol: 5.6%

Erdinger Dunkel, meaning 'dark', gets its dark orange-brown colour from the use of dark malts. The brew has a fruity nose of apples with a faint chocolate note. There is a touch of roastiness in the mouth with fruitiness that is also evident on the finish, joined by a mild hint of chocolate. A very approachable beer in the light Erdinger style, not as strongly flavoured as other interpretations.
Distributed by Noreast Beers.

ERDINGER WEISSBIER KRISTALLKLAR

Privatbrauerei Erdinger Weissbrau, Erding, Germany
South German filtered wheat beer, Alcohol: 5.3%

This is the filtered version of Erdinger and is therefore clear in appearance. It pours a golden colour with the usual wheat beer blossoming head. It has an inviting nose of tropical fruit, vanilla and bubblegum. There is a delicate fruitiness and smoothness on the palate and the finish is sherbety and crisp. This is a good 'crystal clear' wheat beer, clean and quenching.
Distributed by Noreast Beers.

FRANZISKANER HEFE-WEISSBIER

**Spaten-Franziskaner-Bräu,
Munich, Germany
South German unfiltered wheat beer
Alcohol: 5.0%**

This wheat beer is named after the Franciscan monastery that stood close by the original brewery, which itself dates back as far 1363. The original brewery was acquired by Josef Sedlmayr in the mid-1800s and he eventually merged it with his brother Gabriel's Spaten Brewery. Brewing was subsequently transferred to the Spaten Brewery in the 1920s. Franziskaner is an orangey-coloured beer with a yeast haziness. It has a classic wheat beer nose of bubblegum, banana and cloves. The palate is fruity and spicy with a slight yeast bite, more fruit and spice are discernible on the finish. The finish is very quenching in this classic of the style.
Distributed by Blaney Wines.

GAFFEL KÖLSCH

**Privatbrauerei Gaffel Becker & Co.,
Cologne, Germany
Kölsch, Alcohol: 4.8%**

Kölsch beer looks like a lager but is in fact an ale. The term 'Kölsch' is also the best protected name in the world of beer. 'Kölsch' means 'from Cologne' and in 1986, the city's twenty or so Kölsch brewers signed a convention stating that a beer using the name 'Kölsch' could only be made in Cologne, which was ratified by the German Parliament. Gaffel Kölsch can trace its history back to a brewery on the site in 1302. The brewery is currently owned by the Becker family who acquired it in 1908. Gaffel is pale gold in colour and has a delicately fruity nose with a touch of earthiness. The palate is soft, also delicately fruity with a hint of spice. There is a restrained bitterness on the finish and some tart hops, leaving Gaffel refreshing and light – characteristics that are typical of the Kölsch style.
Distributed by Blaney Wines.

GOLDEN PIPPIN

**Copper Dragon Brewery, Skipton,
England
Golden Ale, Alcohol: 4.2%**

The Copper Dragon Brewery is of recent vintage. It was set up in 2003 to give back to the people of Skipton in North Yorkshire what the global brewers had taken away, a pint of the local beer. Golden ale is one of the newer beer styles in England, devised for the warmer days of summer and to compete with lager. Golden Pippin is light gold in colour with a strong citrus nose and a hint of vanilla. The palate is also fruity whilst the finish is mellow and refreshing with a light hop bitterness. Golden Pippin is not as bitter as some interpretations of golden ale but remains a very enjoyable beer.
Distributed by Blaney Wines.

KIRIN ICHIBAN

**Brewed under licence by Charles Wells,
Bedford, England
Japanese lager' Alcohol: 5.0%**

Kirin can trace its history back to 1885 when the Japan Brewery Company was set up – a forerunner of Kirin. By 1888 Kirin Lager was being sold. Kirin Ichiban was launched in the early 1990s, 'Ichiban' meaning 'the best'. It is brewed using corn and rice as well as malted barley, but only the first runnings of wort from the mash tun are used before any boiling water is added to flush out the remaining sugars, making this wort highly concentrated in flavour and sugars. Kirin entered into an agreement with English brewer Charles Wells in 1993 to produce Kirin Ichiban for the European market. Kirin Ichiban is pale straw in colour and has an aroma of sweetcorn with a light floral undercurrent. There is some tangy hop on the palate as well as a hint of citrus and the finish has a refreshing, drying, spicy hop bitterness. Kirin Ichiban is an excellent richly flavoured lager.

Distributed by Premier Beers.

KÖNIG PILSENER

Bitburger Braugruppe, König Brauerei, Duisberg, Germany
German-style Pilsner, Alcohol: 4.9%

Although König is German for 'King', there is no royal connection to this brewery. The name König comes from Theodor König, the brewery's founder in 1848. The brewery has gone through a few hands since then, including the Holsten Group, but from 2004 it has become a wholly-owned subsidiary of the Bitburger Brewing Group. König is a straw coloured beer with a nose of mown hay, cornflour and pine hop notes. The beer is tangy in the mouth with some spicy hop notes and the merest tinge of malt sweetness. The finish is tart and drying, making König a good German-style pilsner.

Distributed by Blaney Wines.

KÖSTRITZER SCHWARTZBIER

Bitburg Braugruppe, Köstritzer Schwartzbierbrauerei, Bad Köstritz, Germany
Black Lager, Alcohol: 4.8%

Although Köstritzer looks like a stout, it is actually a lager. Germany, especially Bavaria, makes dark lagers, known as 'dunkel', but these are dark brown, unlike Köstritzer which is opaque and almost black with dark ruby highlights. The present brewery dates from 1907 and was nationalised under the old East German communist government. When Germany was reunited it was badly run down. Many German and global brewers made moves to

snap up breweries in the former East Germany but things were rather different with Köstritzer. It became part of the Bitburger Brewing Group because one of Bitburger's key men, Dr Axel Simon, remembered drinking the beer in his youth and, out of affection, was determined to bring it back to its former glory, a move that required massive investment. The beer has a nose of malt loaf and black coffee; a roasty, bitter chocolate palate followed by dark chocolate; burnt currants and a delicate but persistent bitterness in the finish. Kostritzer is one of the world's classic beers; drink and enjoy – it is lager but not as most people know it!

Distributed by Blaney Wines

KROMBACHER PILS

Krombacher Brauerei, Kreuztal-Krombach, Germany, German pilsner-style lager, Alcohol: 4.8%

The Krombacher brewery has been in existence since the discovery in 1803 of excellent soft spring water in the locale which was suited to making beer. The brewery has been in the hands of the Schadeberg family for generations and its flagship beer is Krombacher Pils. The beer is light gold in colour and has a delicate floral nose with some malt character. There is the merest hint of maltiness on the palate and finish but both are dominated by the hop bitterness in this decent interpretation of a German pils.

Distributed by Noreast Beers.

KRUŠOVICE IMPERIAL

Gruppe Radeberger, Královský Pivovar Krušovice, Krušovice, Czech Republic
Czech Pilsner-style lager, Alcohol: 5.0%

The Royal Brewery of Krušovice was established as long ago as 1517. It has gone through a number of owners, from the Czech Royal Family in 1583 to the Czech

Soviet Socialist Republic in 1945 when the brewery was nationalised, and is now part of Germany's Radeberger Group. It cannot be called a pilsner as, in the Czech Republic, only beer from Plzen can use that appellation. The beer is pale gold in colour, has good malt character on the nose with grassy and citrus notes. The palate is rounded, full-bodied, bitter and spicy. There is an excellent level of bitterness on the finish which is dry and spicy. This is an excellent Czech lager and has the expected great, crisp bitterness.

Distributed by Richmond Marketing.

LECH PREMIUM

Kompania Piwowarska, Lech Browary, Poznan, Poland
Polish lager, Alcohol: 5.2%

Lech Premium is one of many Polish beers on the market. Kompania Piwowarska, or 'Beer Company', was the result of a merger in 1999 between the Lech and Tyskie breweries. The Lech brewery can trace its history back to 1872 and went through a period of state ownership during the Poland's Communist period. The company is now part of the global giant SAB/Miller. Lech Premium is a straw-coloured lager with a grassy, hay-like nose and an underpinning of malt. The palate is soft with a hint of malt sweetness. There is a light but developing bitterness on the finish, making Lech a decent if somewhat unspectacular lager.

Distributed by Premier Beers.

LICHER WEIZEN

Bitburger Braugruppe, Licher Privatbrauerei, Lich, Germany
South German-style Unfiltered Wheat Beer, Alcohol: 5.4%

Licher is the result of two neighbouring breweries merging in 1922; one brewery from Lich – Johann Heinrich Jhring, dating from 1854 – and one from nearby Butzbach – Jakob Melchior, dating from 1858. The Jhring Melchior company survived until 1999 when it became part of Holsten. However, since 2004, it has become part of the Bitburger Brewing Group. Licher pours hazy orange and has a complex nose of sherbet, pear, muted banana and nutmeg. Spice and pears feature in the mouth whilst the finish is lightly spicy and creamy. Licher is a refreshing beer if a fairly light interpretation of the style with a low level of tartness in the finish.

Distributed by Blaney Wines.

MOOSEHEAD LAGER

Moosehead Breweries, St John, New Brunswick and Dartmouth, Nova Scotia, Canada, North American-style Lager, Alcohol: 5.0%

Moosehead is the largest independent brewery in Canada and also the oldest still in existence. It was established in 1867 by the Oland family and the sixth generation of Olands work there today. The lager pours a pale straw colour and has an aroma of new mown hay with possibly a hint of fruit. The beer is crisp and clean on the palate with a delicate spicy hop finish. Moosehead is a decent lager very much in the inoffensive but lightly flavoured North American style.

Distributed by Premier Beers.

OKOCIM

Okocim Browary, Brzesko, Poland
Polish lager, Alcohol: 5.5%

The Okocim Brewery was established by an Austrian who settled in the area in 1845. After the fall of communism, many breweries in Eastern Europe became targets for the brewing multinationals. In Okocim's case it is the Danish giant Carlsberg that has a large stake in the company. Okocim pours a straw colour and has mown hay, some malt and a little hint of fruit on the nose.

The palate enjoys a good hop character with a malty undercurrent. The finish is balanced, crisp and moderately hoppy, bringing about a very enjoyable lager in the pilsner style.
Distributed by Blaney Wines.

RADEBERGER PILSNER

Radeberger Gruppe, Radeberger Exportbierbrauerei, Radeberg, Germany
German-style Pilsner, Alcohol: 4.8%
Radeberger Pilsner comes, of course, from Radeberg, a town to the north east of Dresden. The brewery traces its history back to 1872 and was the beer of the Royal House of Saxony. The beer is lightish-gold in colour and has a good perfumy hop aroma with a touch of malt. On the palate the beer is crisp, bitter, with some balancing maltiness. The finish is long and bitter which makes it a good interpretation of the style – crisp and refreshing.
Distributed by Richmond Marketing.

SCHÖFFERHOFER HEFEWEIZEN

Radeberger Gruppe, Binding-Brauerei, Frankfurt am Main, Germany
South German-style unfiltered wheat beer, Alcohol: 5.0%
Schöfferhofer is part of Germany's Radeberger Group and has been brewed since 1978. It was one of the first wheat beers of the South German style to be brewed outside this region. It pours a hazy orange-gold colour with a blossoming head. It has the classic bubblegum/banana nose of the style, joined by pears and tart fruit. The palate is soft with fruit and spice. There is some tartness and spice on the finish but it is less tart than some interpretations of the style. It is nevertheless a very enjoyable and quenching wheat beer.
Distributed by Richmond Marketing.

SIERRA NEVADA
Pale ale

Sierra Nevada Brewing Co, Chico, California, USA, Bottle-conditioned Pale Ale,
Alcohol: 5.6%
Sierra Nevada brewed their first batch of beer in 1980. The company was formed by two men with a passion for home brewing – Ken Grossman and Paul Camusi. Sierra Nevada was one of the first in a wave of craft brewing that has seen the establishment of countless breweries across the US. The pale ale is a classic: amber in colour, with a strong aromatic citrus hop nose that is dominated by grapefruit from the Cascade hops and backed by a slightly earthy quality. Citrus dominates the palate and the drying, robustly bitter, lengthy finish. Sierra Nevada Pale Ale is a perfect introduction to the US craft brewing scene of fully-flavoured beer that is a million miles away from the tasteless fizzy lager that is usually associated with the United States.
Distributed by Blaney Wines.

SINGHA

Boon Rawd Group, Pathum Thani Brewery, Pathum Thani, Thailand
Pilsner-style lager, Alcohol: 6.0%
Singha is named after a mythical creature that looks rather like a lion. The brewery was established in 1933 by Phraya Bhirom-Bhakdi and a German brewer was recruited to devise the recipes. The Bhirom-Bhakdi family still operate the brewery and the Germanic tradition is still evident in the character of the beer. The beer has an almost orangey aroma and whilst there is a hint of fruitiness on the palate it is dominated by a robust hoppy tang. The crisp, mouth-drying finish has an excellent quenching bitterness with a hint of citric fruit. Singha is an exceptional beer in two

senses. Firstly, most lagers brewed outside the historic brewing nations tend to be inoffensive thirst-quenchers; Singha, however, is fully flavoured. Secondly, it is exceptional as it is an excellent lager and up there with some of the best.
Distributed by Premier Beers.

SPATEN

Spaten-Franziskaner-Bräu, Munich, Germany, Helles, Alcohol: 5.2%

Hell is German for light but in beer terms it does not refer to the alcohol level. Gabriel Sedlmayr, whose family acquired the Spaten brewery in 1807, produced the world's first lager beer in the first half of the 1800s. This lager was dark-brown in colour as malting techniques had not advanced sufficiently to be able to produce lightly cured malt. However, by the end of that century, Spaten were producing a blonde lager and the term 'hell' or 'helles' was used to differentiate it from the 'dunkel', or dark, lagers. Although Spaten is now a public company, the Sedlmayrs still retain a large stake. Spaten Hell is pale gold in colour and has a nose accented towards malt with a light fruitiness and some perfumey aromas. The beer is soft and smooth on the palate, the finish has a light bitterness and is delicately dry. Helles are less hoppy and bitter than a pilsner and Spaten is an excellent introduction to the style.
Distributed by Blaney Wines.

SPITFIRE

Shepherd Neame Brewery, Faversham, Kent, England

English bitter, Alcohol: 4.5%

Named after the World War Two fighter plane that duelled with the German Luftwaffe in the skies over Kent in the 'Battle of Britain'. It was originally launched for the RAF Benevolent Fund in 1990 on the occasion of the 50th Anniversary of the Battle of Britain but is now a staple beer. Autumnal amber in colour, it has a rich, spicy aroma with dark fruit notes. In the mouth it is rounded with a spicy and tangy hop character and a long, lingering finish. Spitfire is a rich and satisfying ale and it is easy to see why, since its launch, it has become a very popular ale indeed.
Distributed by Noreast Beers.

TYSKIE GRONIE

Kompania Piwowarska, Browary Tyskie, Tyche, Poland

Polish lager, Alcohol: 5.6%

Tyskie Brewery joined Lech to create the Kompania Piwowarska, which is now owned by SAB/Miller. Tyskie is the older of the two companies, with reports of brewing in the town dating back as far as 1613. Tyskie is light gold in colour and has a perfumy mown hay aroma with some delicate fruity notes. The flavour is more malty than would be expected, resulting in a bitter-sweet, crisp palate and finish. There is also a good smack of hop bitterness in the finish, making Tyskie a very good and enjoyable lager. Distributed by Premier Beers.

WHITSTABLE BAY ORGANIC ALE

Shepherd Neame Brewery, Faversham, Kent, England

Organic English bitter, Alcohol: 4.5%

Whitstable Bay Organic Ale is brewed with local organic malt, Gem and Hallertauer organic hops from New Zealand and is also vegetarian friendly. The beer is an amber colour and has a citrus nose – mainly oranges – together with some earthy hops. Bitter, fruity and malty on the palate, there is more citrus in the finish and a good degree of hop bitterness. A very good ale and if you are into organic food, here is the

beer to match.
Distributed by Noreast Beers.

Major beer importers

Blaney Wines, No. 6, Unit 23, Pennybridge
Industrial Estate, Ballymena BT42 2HB
T/F: +44 (0)28 2564 0816

Noreast Beers, Coes Road Industrial Estate,
Dundalk, County Louth
T: +353 (0)42 9339858
F: +353 (0)42 9336370
E: sales@noreastbeers.ie

Premier International Beers, Clonard,
Enfield, Count Meath
T: +353 (0)44 9375312
E: sales@premierbeers.ie

Richmond Marketing, 1st Floor Harmony
Court, Harmony Row, Dublin 2
T: +353 (0) 1 631 6100
F: +353 (0) 1 639 4882
W: www.richmondmarketing.com
E: reception@richmondmarketing.com

Adjuncts

Ingredients added to barley malt in the mash, such as rice and maize (corn). They can be added for reasons of cheapness, to make the beer lighter in flavour or to produce a special flavour in the final beer. Brewing sugars and syrups are also adjuncts but are added in the brew kettle.

Ale

Originally denoted a malted alcoholic drink with herbs and spices added. Now covers all beers fermented at warm temperatures including stouts and wheat beers.

Alpha Acid

Acid in the cone of the hop plant that produces bitterness in beer.

Aroma hops

See 'late hops'.

Base cider

Matured cider that will be used as the base for the finished product. Base ciders from different maturation vats are often blended to make the final product.

Beer

Interchangeable with ale until the appearance of hops when it came to denote a hopped drink as distinct from unhopped 'ale'. Now used to cover all drinks made from fermented grains, mainly barley malt, that have been hopped. Includes all ales and lagers.

Bittering hops

See 'kettle hops'.

Bittersharps

Apples high in acid and tannin.

Bittersweets

Apples low in acid but high in tannin.

Bottle-conditioning

Beer or cider that is bottled with live yeast so that it undergoes a secondary fermentation (conditioning) in the bottle creating a natural sparkle.

Brew kettle

Also known as a 'copper'. The vessel in which wort is boiled and hops are added.

Brewpub

A pub or restaurant that brews its own beer on the premises.

Burtonisation

The addition of mineral salts to the brewing liquor similar to those found in the hard water of Burton-on-Trent.

Carbonation

The sparkle in a beer or cider created by carbon dioxide (CO_2). Cask-conditioned ale and bottle-conditioned beer and cider have a natural carbonation from the live yeast in the cask or bottle. More commonly it is injected into the keg or bottle in a 50:50 ratio with nitrogen or is the result of the dispensing system in the bar or pub.

Cask ale

Also known as 'real ale'. A draught beer that is put into cask with some live yeast so that the beer undergoes a secondary fermentation in the cask creating a natural sparkle. The beer conditions to maturity in the pub cellar due to the natural working of the yeast.

Cask-conditioning

Putting beer into a cask in an unfinished state with live yeast so that it undergoes a secondary fermentation (conditioning) in the cask creating a natural sparkle.

Chaptelisation

Increasing the fermentable material by adding sugar to apple juice to get a higher level of alcohol at the end of fermentation.

Cheese

A layer of apple pulp wrapped in cloth during the pressing stage of cidermaking. Cheeses are set one on top of another and then pressed. The juice flows out whilst the solids are retained in the cloth.

Conditioning

Period of maturation that rids beer and cider of rough alcohols and develops the flavour and carbonation.

Conversion

Process that happens during mashing whereby enzymes convert the starch in the grist into fermentable malt sugar.

Cool-fermentation

Also known as bottom-fermentation. Fermentation taking place at a low temperature, usually used for lagers, with yeast sinking to the bottom of the vessel.

Craft brewery

Also known as a 'microbrewery'. A small brewery that brews batches of beer often for local distribution. Part of a generation of new small breweries that have sprung up worldwide since the mid 1970s but did not really begin in Ireland until the mid 1990s with some exceptions.

Esters

Volatile flavour compounds created during fermentation. They often produce a fruity aroma and taste in the finished beer and are mainly associated with the ale family of beer. Can also be found in cider.

Fermentation

Also known as 'primary fermentation'. Stage in the brewing and cidermaking process where yeast is added turning malt sugars in wort or fruit sugars in apple juice into alcohol and carbon dioxide.

Finings

Liquid added to beer that attracts yeast particles and sinks to the bottom clarifying the beer. Isinglass and Irish moss are the most common finings. Isinglass is made with the bladders of the sturgeon fish whilst Irish moss (Carrageen) is a type of seaweed.

Finished beer

Beer that has been conditioned and is ready to drink.

Finished cider

A cider that has been 'made up' to

conform with the final product specification and is ready to drink.

Green beer

A raw form of beer emerging after fermentation but not yet ready to drink as it contains rough alcohols.

Green malt

Barley that has germinated but not yet been kilned.

Grist

A rough flour made from milling barley malt and other grains prior to mashing.

Hop back

A vessel with a perforated base used for separating hopped wort from the petals of the hop flowers. Used by breweries using whole cone hops.

Hopped wort

Liquid run off from the brew kettle that has been boiled and hops added ready for fermentation.

Hops

A climbing plant whose cones contain acids and resins that gives aroma and bitterness to beer whilst also helping to prevent bacterial infection. Brewers use whole cones, pellets or hop extract.

Infusion

Simplest form of mashing. The grist is soaked in hot brewing liquor so that enzymes in the malt convert the starch to sugar.

Kegging

Putting beer or cider that has been filtered and into a sealed keg under pressure. Unlike cask ale it is a finished product and will not condition or develop any further.

Kettle Hops

Also known as 'bittering hops'. Hops varieties high in alpha acids that are added at the start of the boil to impart bitterness and dryness in the finished beer.

Lager

The German word for 'store' and comes from a traditional German practice of storing, or 'lagering', beer for months in cool caves during which a secondary fermentation will take place leaving a crisp and clean finished beer. Now denotes a beer fermented and conditioned at low temperatures. Often pale but can be any colour with a clean, quenching taste.

Late Hops

Also known as 'aroma hops'. Hop varieties low in alpha acids that are added towards the end of the boil to impart aroma in the finished beer.

Lauter tun

From the German word meaning 'to clarify'. A vessel with a perforated base used to clarify wort after mashing. It has sharp rakes allowing for a very thorough extraction of malt sugars from the mash.

Liquor

Purified water used for mashing in the brewery.

Making up

Process in cidermaking after maturation is complete where the cider is brought up to its final specification. Making up can include blending ciders from different maturation vats, adding water to bring the alcoholic strength down, injecting carbon dioxide, adding sugar to get a sweet cider and adding colouring for consistency across batches.

Malo-lactic fermentation

A natural process that may occur during the maturation of cider. Lactic acid bacteria convert harsh malic acid in the raw cider into less harsh lactic acid and carbon dioxide and the resulting finished cider will be less sharp. Cidermakers may encourage this process by adding strains of bacteria, others will take steps to prevent it from happening.

Malting

Process taking place at a Maltings where grain – usually barley – is steeped in water, partially germinated and heated to dryness. This modifies the grain so that its reserves of starch become accessible for the brewer.

Mashing

The first stage in the brewing process where grist and hot brewing liquor is mixed in a mash tun. The starches in the grist convert into fermentable sugars

and the resultant liquid is known as wort.

Mash tun

Vessel in which grist is mixed with hot brewing liquor to start the brewing process.

Maturation

Period needed for raw cider to purge itself of rough alcohols and during which it may undergo a malo-lactic fermentation.

Milling

Rough chopping of apples or pears to aid juice extraction.

Modification

Process that happens during malting whereby a grain of barley is modified so that its starch is made accessible to the brewer.

Nitrogenation

Carbonation using a high proportion of nitrogen – usually around 75% - in the gas mixture. Nitogenated beers have a smooth mouthfeel and thick creamy head achieved by using a special tap in the bar or pub. Bottles and cans can also be nitrogenated but need to have a 'widget' added to achieve the same results. Nitrogenation usually somewhat diminishes the flavour of beer.

Pasteurisation

Named after Louis Pasteur and involves heating filtered beer to kill off any remaining yeast cells and bacteria to microbiologically stabilise the product.

Pasteurised beer has a longer shelf life but often loses some flavour in the process. Pasteur himself developed the method to protect wine but said that beer was too delicate to be treated in this way.

Pomace

Dry apple pulp that has been pressed and the juice run off. Can also be applied to milled apple pulp before pressing.

Pressing

Stage in cidermaking where the juice is extracted from apple pulp.

Racking

Separating green beer or raw cider from spent yeast by pumping it into conditioning tanks or maturation vats. For cask-conditioned beer, racking refers to putting the beer into casks.

Raw cider

Cider after fermentation that is not yet ready to drink as it contains rough alcohols.

Secondary fermentation

Happens during the conditioning of beer or maturation of cider. Residual quantities of yeast will create a secondary fermentation that will develop the flavour and condition of beer and helps mature cider. Will happen in the cask in a cask-conditioned beer or in bottle for a bottle-conditioned beer or cider.

Sharps

Apples high in acid but low in tannin.

Sparging

From the French word esparger meaning 'to sprinkle'. After the mash is finished, the grains are sprayed with hot water to rinse out any remaining malt sugars.

Sweets

Apples low in acid and tannin.

Trub

Residue left at the end of the boil containing proteins and other matter.

Tun

Originally denoted a large vessel for storing beer. Now used to denote certain brewing vessels.

Warm-fermentation

Also known as top-fermentation. Fermentation taking place at a relatively warm temperature, usually used for members of the ale family, with the yeast rising to the surface forming a thick head of foam.

Whirlpool

Device often at the bottom of the brew kettle that swirls the hopped wort to separate it from the remains of hops and any trub.

Wort

Pronounced 'wurt'. Sweet liquid run off from the mash or lauter tun rich in malt sugars.

Yeast

A natural fungus that attacks sweet liquids such as wort or apple juice and converts the sugar into alcohol and carbon dioxide.

PICTURE CREDITS

Iorwerth Griffiths: 29, 39 (bottles), 43, 44, 47, 48, 49, 50, 51 (main picture), 52, 53, 54, 56 (picture), 57, 60, 61, 62, 63, 72, 73 (bottles), 74 (bottle), 77, 78, 89, 92, 94 (main picture), 97, 99, 100 (bottle), 101, 102, 103, 112, 114, 115, 126, 130 (bottle), 138, 139, 140, 142, 143.

C & C Group plc/Grayling: 123, 131, 132, 133, 134, 135, 136, 137.

Armagh Cider Company Ltd.: 129, 130.

Dave Jones (Cymdeithas Perai a Seidr Cymru/Welsh Cider and Perry Society): 122, 124, 125, 142.

National Hop Association of England: 25, 26, 27, 28, 120.

Whitewater Brewing Company: 116, 118, 119.

Strangford Lough Brewing Company: 113.

Porterhouse Brewing Company: 104, 105, 106, 107, 108.

Messrs Maguires: 99 (logo), 100 (logo).

Kinsale Brewing Company: 94 (logo), 95, 96.

Hooker Brewing Company: 90, 91.

Hilden Brewing Company 84, 85, 86, 97, 88.

Heineken Ireland: 79, 80, 81, 82, 83.

Guinness Archive & Diageo: 12, 13, 14, 16, 17, 67, 68, 69, 70, 73 (picture), 74 (main picture).

Franciscan Well: 64, 65, 66.

College Green Brewery: 58, 59.

Celtic Brew: 55, 56 (beer pack).

Carlow Brewing Company: 51 (logo).

Biddy Early: 46.

Beamish and Crawford plc: 10, 40, 41, 45.

Arainn Mhor Brewing Company: 37, 38, 39 (pic).

Greencore Malt: 11, 30, 32.